HTML & CSS

Programming Guide

First Edition

Venkatesh Ramasamy

Lulu Press, Inc.
3101 Hillsborough Street
Raleigh, North Carolina, 27607
United States of America

HTML & CSS Programming Guide, First Edition

by Venkatesh Ramasamy

International Standard Book Number (ISBN): 978-1-304-69978-7

ISBN 978-1-304-69978-7

9 781304 699787

90000

Printed in the United States of America.

First Edition published on December 2013.

Disclaimer

Printed and bounded in Lulu Press, Inc., 3101 Hillsborough Street, Raleigh, North Carolina, 27607, United States of America.

Preface

The Hyper-Text Markup Language and the World Wide Web altered the face of the internet and are evolving at near-light speed, bringing the promise of a seamless Internet ever closer to reality. The internet has grown to touch more and more lives every day. In addition, the multimedia content that can be provided via HTML and CSS makes the web an exciting to be. The number of possibilities for providing information and content over the web is astounding, and its growing every day. This book titled, HTML & CSS Programming Guide comprehensively teaches and documents the basic standards for coding web pages. It details the technologies used in building a web page and covers the basic structure and formatting to create a static and dynamic page on the Internet. The tight focus on these key standards allows maximum coverage and examples to best show readers how to put them to work. This book is the single source you need to get up quickly get up to speed and greatly enhance your skill and knowledge in providing information on the World Wide Web.

This book is organized into three parts along with practical examples that will show you how to structure your data correctly using HTML, along with styling and layout basics using Cascading Style Sheets (CSS).

- **Part I - HTML:** The first part is explained with fifteen chapters including the concepts like texts, fonts, images, lists, links, tables, audio, video, forms, frames, layers, scripting, etc in HTML programming.

- **Part II - CSS:** The second part is explained with sixteen chapters including the concepts like fonts, texts, lists, links, background styles, borders, outlines, margins, padding styles, dimensions, boxes, positions, floating styles, marquees, color styles, etc in CSS programming.

- **Part III - HTML & CSS Reference:** The third part is explained with eight chapters including the concepts like color names, hex values, ASCII & ISO character sets, symbols entities, language codes, events, measurements values, etc in HTML & CSS reference guides.

This book is written for anyone who wants to learn how to create web pages, and for people who may have dabbled in writing web pages, but who want to really understand the languages of the web, to give them more control over the pages they create. More experienced web developers can also benefit from this book because it teaches some of the latest technologies and encourages you to embrace web standards that not only meet the needs of the new devices that access the web, but also help make your sites available to more visitors. You don't need any previous programming experience to work with this book. This is one of the first steps on the programming ladder. Whether you are just a hobbyist or want to make a career of web programming, this book will teach you the basics of programming for the web. Happy Reading !!

About Programming Guide Series:

The titles in this programming guide series deals with technical descriptions of important software programming languages to give insights on how programming works and what it can be used for. These are ideal first books for beginners from a wide range of backgrounds like enterprise developer, technical manager, solution architect, tester, etc. This is an ideal place to begin mastering a new programming area and lay a solid foundation for further study. The curriculum of these books is carefully designed to reflect the needs of a diverse population, so there is something for everyone. The books in this programming guide series cover a broad range of topics including ANSI C, HTML, CSS, JavaScript, VBScript, JCL, VSAM, etc.

Warm Regards,
Venkatesh Ramasamy
twitter @rvenkateshbe

Author

Venkatesh Ramasamy is a senior quality engineer and technology consultant for a leading multinational company in Information Technology sector. He has excellent experience in managing enterprise IT project life cycle and has developed many software products for providing end-to-end IT services with optimized cost and improved quality. He is also vastly experienced in working with large insurers and financial services organizations based out of UK & US, for setting up independent test centers for their enterprise level quality engineering needs. He has very much interested in programming languages & web design technologies and has helped in developing wide variety of software products for the customers to successfully implement their new age corporate IT strategies.

Over the years he has presented and published many whitepapers at both national and international conferences and has also authored various technical articles in international magazines. He is also the author of several other programming books including ANSI C Programming Guide, HTML & CSS Programming Guide, JavaScript Programming Guide, JCL & VSAM Programming Guide and Handbook on 1000 Software Testing Tools.

You can reach him at his Twitter handle @rvenkateshbe.

Contents

Part: I - HTML

Part: II - CSS

Part: III - Appendix

PART - I

HTML

Programming

HTML & CSS

Programming Guide

Chapter 01

Introduction

01. Introduction

HTML - Hyper Text Markup Language is the predominant markup language for designing web pages. It provides a means to describe the structure of text-based information in a document - by denoting certain text as links, headings, paragraphs, lists, and so on - and to supplement that text with interactive forms, embedded images, and other objects. HTML is written in the form of tags, surrounded by angle brackets. An HTML file is a text file containing small markup tags HTML can also describe, to some degree, the appearance and semantics of a document, and can include embedded scripting language code which can affect the behavior of Web browsers and other HTML processors. HTML is error free and case insensitive language.

Brief History of HTML:

HTML was originally developed by Tim Berners-Lee while at CERN, and popularized by the Mosaic browser developed at NCSA. During the course of the 1990s it has blossomed with the explosive growth of the Web. During this time, HTML has been extended in a number of ways. The Web depends on Web page authors and vendors sharing the same conventions for HTML. This has motivated joint work on specifications for HTML.

HTML 2.0 (November 1995) was developed under the aegis of the Internet Engineering Task Force (IETF) to codify common practice in late 1994. HTML+ (1993) and HTML 3.0 (1995) proposed much richer versions of HTML. Despite never receiving consensus in standards discussions, these drafts led to the adoption of a range of new features. The efforts of the World Wide Web Consortium's HTML Working Group to codify common practice in 1996 resulted in HTML 3.2 (January 1997).

HTML 4 (April 1997) extends HTML with mechanisms for style sheets, scripting, frames, embedding objects, improved support for right to left and mixed direction text, richer tables, and enhancements to forms, offering improved accessibility for people with disabilities.

HTML has been developed with the vision that all manner of devices should be able to use information on the Web: PCs with graphics displays of varying resolution and color depths, cellular telephones, hand held devices, devices for speech for output and input, computers with high or low bandwidth, and so on.

Working with HTML Documents

We can view an HTML file in a Web browser (Internet Explorer, Netscape, Firefox, etc) by opening it with the Open command in the File menu. When developing a Web page, it's convenient to keep the Web browser and the HTML file open in a text editor at the same time. If we want to make a change, click on the text editor window, edit the HTML text, Save it, then click on the Web browser window and click on the Reload button.

Creating an HTML document is easy. To begin coding HTML we need only two things: a simple-text editor and a web browser. Notepad is the most basic of simple-text editors and we will probably code a fair amount of HTML with it.

Here are the simple steps to create a basic HTML document:

- Open Notepad or another text editor.
- At the top of the page type <html>.
- On the next line, indent five spaces and now add the opening header tag: <head>.
- On the next line, indent ten spaces and type <title> </title>.
- Go to the next line, indent five spaces from the margin and insert the closing header tag: </head>.
- Five spaces in from the margin on the next line, type<body>.
- Now drop down another line and type the closing tag right below its mate: </body>.
- Finally, go to the next line and type </html>.
- In the File menu, choose Save As.
- In the Save as Type option box, choose All Files.
- Name the file template.htm.
- Click Save.

We have basic HTML document now, to see some result put the following code in title and body tags.

```
<html>
<head>
<title>This is document title</title>
</head>
<body>
<h1>This is a heading</h1>
<p>Document description goes here.....</p>
</body>
</html>
```

Now we have created one HTML page and we can use a Web Browser to open this HTML file to see the result. Web Pages are nothing but they are simple HTML files with some content which can be rendered using Web Browsers.

Here <html>, <head>,...<p>, <h1> etc. are called HTML tags. HTML tags are building blocks of an HTML document and we will learn all the HTML tags in subsequent chapters. HTML file can have extension as .htm or .html. So we can use either of them based on comfort.

HTML Document Structure

An HTML document starts and ends with <html> and </html> tags. These tags tell the browser that the entire document is composed in HTML. Inside these two tags, the document is split into two sections:

- The <head>...</head> elements, which contain information about the document such as title of the document, author of the document etc. Information inside this tag does not display outside.

- The <body>...</body> elements, which contain the real content of the document that can see on the screen.

HTML Tags and Elements

HTML language is a markup language and we use many tags to markup text. In the above example we have seen <html>, <body> etc. are called HTML tags or HTML elements.

Every tag consists of a tag name, sometimes followed by an optional list of tag attributes, all placed between opening and closing brackets (< and >). The simplest tag is nothing more than a name appropriately enclosed in brackets, such as <head> and <i>. More complicated tags contain one or more attributes, which specify or modify the behavior of the tag. According to the HTML standard, tag and attribute names are not case-sensitive. There's no difference in effect between <head>, <Head>, <HEAD>, or even <HeaD>; they are all equivalent.

HTML Elements

HTML documents are composed entirely of HTML elements that, in their most general form have three components: a pair of tags, a "start tag" and "end tag"; some attributes within the start tag; and finally, any textual and graphical content between the start and end tags, perhaps including other nested elements. The HTML element is everything between and including the start and end tags. Each tag is enclosed in angle brackets.

The general form of an HTML element is therefore: <tag attribute1="value1" attribute2="value2">content</tag>. Some HTML elements are defined as empty elements and take the form <tag attribute1="value1" attribute2="value2" >. Empty elements may enclose no content, for instance, the BR tag or the inline IMG tag. The name of an HTML element is the name used in the tags. Note that the end tag's name is preceded by a slash character, "/", and that in empty elements the end tag is neither required nor allowed. If attributes are not mentioned, default values are used in each case.

HTML Attributes

Attributes are another important part of HTML markup. An attribute is used to define the characteristics of an element and is placed inside the element's opening tag. All attributes are made up of two parts: a name and a value:

- The name is the property we want to set. For example, the <font> element in the example carries an attribute whose name is face, which we can use to indicate which typeface we want the text to appear in.

- The value is what we want the value of the property to be. The first example was supposed to use the Arial typeface, so the value of the face attribute is Arial.

The value of the attribute should be put in double quotation marks, and is separated from the name by the equals sign. We can see that a color for the text has been specified as well as the typeface in this <font> element:

```
<font face="arial" color="#CC0000">
```

Here's a table of generic attributes that are readily usable with many of HTML's tags.

Attribute	Options	Function
align	right, left, center	Horizontally aligns tags
valign	top, middle, bottom	Vertically aligns tags within an HTML element
bgcolor	numeric, hexidecimal, RGB values	Places a background color behind an element
background	URL	Places an background image behind an element
id	User Defined	Names an element for use with Cascading Style Sheets
class	User Defined	Classifies an element for use with Cascading Style Sheets.
width	Numeric Value	Specifies the width of tables, images, or table cells
height	Numeric Value	Specifies the height of tables, images, or table cells
title	User Defined	"Pop-up" title for elements

HTML & CSS

Programming Guide

Chapter 02

Basic Tags

02. Basic Tags

`<html>...</html>`	It defines the entire web page.
`<head>...</head>`	It defines the web page head section.
`<title>...</title>`	It defines the web page title section.
`<body>...</body>`	It defines the main body of the web page (visible content). *Attributes:* • bgcolor - used to provide background color. • text - used to provide text color. • link - used to provide color to the hyperlink. • alink - used to provide color to active link. • vlink - used to provide color to visited link. • background - used to provide the background image.
`<!... Comment ...>`	It defines the commented lines in the web page script. The commented lines are not visible in the rendered web page.

Coding Snippets:

Program 2.1

Usage of <html>, <head>, <title> tags

```
<html>
<head>
<title>This is the title tag</title>
</head>
</html>
```

Program 2.2

Usage of <body> tag

```
<html>
<head>
```

```
<title>Page with body tag</title>
</head>
<body>
Welcome to HTML Programming !!
</body>
</html>
```

Program 2.3

Usage of <body> tag bgcolor, text attributes

```
<html>
<head>
<title>Page with background color</title>
</head>
<body bgcolor="yellow" text="#ff00ff">
Welcome to HTML Programming !!
</body>
</html>
```

Program 2.4

Usage of <body> tag background attribute

```
<html>
<head>
<title>Page with background image</title>
</head>
<body background="image1.jpg">
Welcome to HTML Programming !!
</body>
</html>
```

HTML & CSS

Programming Guide

Chapter 03

Texts & Fonts

03. Texts & Fonts

`<b>...</b>`	It defines the bold text.
`<i>...</i>`	It defines the italic text.
`<u>...</u>`	It defines the underlined text.
`<big>...</big>`	It defines the bold text.
`<small>...</small>`	It defines the small sized text.
`<strong>...</strong>`	It defines the important text.
`<em>...</em>`	It defines the emphasized text.
`<sub>...</sub>`	It defines the subscripted text.
`<sup>...</sup>`	It defines the superscripted text.
`<s>...</s>`	It defines the strike-out text.
`<strike>...</strike>`	It defines the strike-out text.
`<ins>...</ins>`	It defines the inserted text.
`<del>...</del>`	It defines the deleted text.
`<tt>...</tt>`	It defines the type writer text.
`<kbd>...</kbd>`	It defines the keyboard text format.
`<code>...</code>`	It defines the computer code text.
`<samp>...</samp>`	It defines the sample computer code.
`<var>...</var>`	It defines the variable text.
`<pre>...</pre>`	It defines the pre-formatted text.
`<dfn>...</dfn>`	It defines the definition term.
`<abbr>...</abbr>`	It defines the abbreviation term.
`<acronym>...</acronym>`	It defines the acronym term.
`<cite>...</cite>`	It defines the citation text.
`<q>...</q>`	It defines the inline quotation.

\<quote\>...\</quote\>	It defines the inline quotation.
\<address\>...\</address\>	It defines the contact information text for the author.
\<blockquote\>... \</blockquote\>	It defines the section which provides margin segment.
\<bdo\>...\</bdo\>	It defines the text direction. *Attributes:* • dir – used to provide the text direction. rtl: right to left; ltr: left to right;
\<blink\>...\</blink\>	It defines the blinking text.
\<basefont\>...\</basefont\>	It defines the basefont text.
\<font\>...\</font\>	It defines the text with different size, face and color. *Attributes:* • size - used to specify the size of the letters. • face - used to specify the font type of letters. • color - used to specify the color of the letters.
\<h1\>...\</h1\> \<h2\>...\</h2\> \<h3\>...\</h3\> \<h4\>...\</h4\> \<h5\>...\</h5\> \<h6\>...\</h6\>	It defines the heading text. \<h1\> defines the most important heading and \<h6\> defines the least important heading. *Attributes:* • align - used to align the headings. left: left alignment; right: right alignment; justify: justify alignment; center: center alignment; • color - used to provide color to the headings.
\<p\>...\</p\>	It defines the paragraph formatted text. It adds margin space automatically before and after each \<p\> element. *Attributes:* • align - used to align the headings. left: left alignment; right: right alignment; justify: justify alignment; center: center alignment;

`<div>...</div>`	It defines the division or a section in the web page.
	Attributes:
	• align - used to specify the alignment.
	  left: left alignment; right: right alignment;
	  justify: justify alignment; center: center
	  alignment;
	• name - used to specify tag name.
	• id - used to specify the tag id.

` ...</br>`	It defines the line break.
`<hr>...</hr>`	It defines the horizontal line break.
` `	It defines the non-breakable space.

Coding Snippets

Program 3.1

Usage of <b>, <i>, <u> tags

```
<html>
<head>
<title>Changing Text Style</title>
</head>
<body background="image1.jpg">
<b>Welcome to HTML Programming !!</b><br />
<i>Welcome to HTML Programming !!</i><br />
<u>Welcome to HTML Programming !!</U><br />
</body>
</html>
```

Program 3.2

Usage of nesting of <b>, <i>, <u> tags

```
<html>
<head>
<title>Nesting Text Style</title>
</head>
<body background="image1.jpg">
```

```
<b>Welcome to HTML Programming !!</b><br />
<b><i>Welcome to HTML Programming !!</i></b><br />
<i><u>Welcome to HTML Programming !!</U></i><br />
</body>
</html>
```

Program 3.3

Usage of <TT> tag

```
<html>
<head>
<title>Typewriter Text</title>
</head>
<body background="image1.jpg">
<TT>Welcome to HTML Programming !!</TT><br />
</body>
</html>
```

Program 3.4

Usage of <font> tag size attribute

```
<html>
<head>
<title>Changing Font Size</title>
</head>
<body>
<font size=1>Sample Text</font><br />
<font size=2>Sample Text</font><br />
<font size=3>Sample Text</font><br />
<font size=4>Sample Text</font><br />
<font size=5>Sample Text</font><br />
<font size=6>Sample Text</font><br />
<font size=7>Sample Text</font><br />
</body>
</html>
```

Program 3.5

Usage of <font> tag size, face attributes

```
<html>
<head>
<title>Changing Font Size and Face</title>
</head>
<body>
<font size=4 face="Arial">Sample Text</font><br />
<font size=4 face="Impact">Sample Text</font><br />
<font size=4 face="Times Roman">Sample Text</font><br />
<font size=4 face="serif">Sample Text</font><br />
<font size=4 face="verdana">Sample Text</font><br />
<font size=4 face="helvetica">Sample Text</font><br />
<font size=4 face="arial">Sample Text</font><br />
</body>
</html>
```

Program 3.6

Usage of <font> tag size, face, color attributes

```
<html>
<head>
<title>Changing Font Size, Face & Color</title>
</head>
<body>
<font size=4 face="Arial" color="#ff0000">Sample Text</font><br />
<font size=4 face="Impact" color="#00ff00">Sample Text</font><br />
<font size=4 face="Times Roman" color="#0000ff">Sample Text</font><br
/>
<font size=4 face="serif" color="red">Sample Text</font><br />
<font size=4 face="verdana" color="green">Sample Text</font><br />
<font size=4 face="helvetica" color="blue">Sample Text</font><br />
<font size=4 face="arial" color="yellow">Sample Text</font><br />
</body>
</html>
```

Program 3.7

Usage of <font> tag size, face, color attributes

```
<html>
<head>
<title>Changing Font Size, Face & Color</title>
</head>
<body>
<font size=4 face="Arial" color="#ff0000">Sample Text</font><br />
<font size=5 face="Impact" color="#00ff00">Sample Text</font><br />
<font size=6 face="Times Roman" color="#0000ff">Sample Text</font><br />
<font size=7 face="serif" color="red">Sample Text</font><br />
<font size=8 face="verdana" color="green">Sample Text</font><br />
<font size=9 face="helvetica" color="blue">Sample Text</font><br />
<font size=10 face="arial" color="yellow">Sample Text</font><br />
</body>
</html>
```

Program 3.8

Usage of <body> tag link, vlink, alink attributes

```
<html>
<head>
<title>Changing default font colors</title>
</head>
<body bgcolor="yellow" text="Black" link="#0000ff" vlink="#00ff00"
alink="#ff0000">
Some Text
<a href="test1.html">Test page:1</a>
</body>
</html>
```

Program 3.9

Usage of heading tags <h1> to <h6>

```
<html>
<head>
```

```
<title>Default Headings Format</title>
</head>
<body>
<h1>First Heading</h1><br />
<h2>Second Heading</h2><br />
<h3>Third Heading</h3><br />
<h4>Fourth Heading</h4><br />
<h5>Fifth Heading</h5><br />
<h6>Sixth Heading</h6><br />
</body>
</html>
```

Program 3.10

Usage of paragraph <p> tag

```
<html>
<head>
<title>Default Headings</title>
</head>
<body>
<h1>About HTML</h1><br />

<p> HTML is written in the form of HTML elements consisting of tags
enclosed in angle brackets, within the web page content. HTML tags most
commonly come in pairs although some tags, known as empty elements,
are unpaired. </p>

<p>The first tag in a pair is the start tag, and the second tag is the end
tag (they are also called opening tags and closing tags). In between these
tags web designers can add text, tags, comments and other types of text-
based content.</p>

</body>
</html>
```

Program 3.11

Usage of <blockquote> tag

```
<html>
<head>
<title>blockquote Tag Example</title>
</head>
<body>
<h1>About HTML</h1><br />
<p> <blockquote> HTML is written in the form of HTML elements
consisting of tags enclosed in angle brackets, within the web page
content. HTML tags most commonly come in pairs although some tags,
known as empty elements, are unpaired. </blockquote></p>

<p> <blockquote> The first tag in a pair is the start tag, and the second
tag is the end tag (they are also called opening tags and closing tags). In
between these tags web designers can add text, tags, comments and
other types of text-based content.</blockquote></p>
</body>
</html>
```

Program 3.12

Usage of <pre> tag

```
<html>
<head>
<title>Pre-Formatted Text</title>
</head>
<body>
<pre>
        India India
         ndia Indi
          dia Ind
           ia In
            a I
</pre>
</body>
</html>
```

Program 3.13

Usage of heading tag align attribute

```
<html>
<head>
<title>Text Alignment Format</title>
</head>
<body>
<h1 align="center">Sample Text</h1>
<h2 align="left"> Sample Text </h2>
<h3 align="right"> Sample Text </h3>
</body>
</html>
```

Program 3.14

Usage of <div> tag

```
<html>
<head>
<title>Formatted Text</title>
</head>
<body>
<h1 align="center">HTML</h1>
<p> HTML is written in the form of HTML elements consisting of tags
enclosed in angle brackets, within the web page content. HTML tags most
commonly come in pairs although some tags, known as empty elements,
are unpaired.</p>
<br /><br />
<div align="right">- Venkatesh Ramasamy</div>
</body>
</html>
```

Program 3.15

Usage of <hr> tag

```
<html>
<head>
<title>Horizontal Rules</title>
```

```
</head>
<body>
<h2>Various of styles of Horizonal Rules</h2><br />
<hr align="center" color="red" width="600">
<hr align="center" color="blue" width="500">
<hr align="center" color="green" width="400">
<hr align="left" color="red" width="300">
<hr align="right" color="blue" width="300">
<hr color="red" >
</body>
</html>
```

Program 3.16
Usage of <dfn> tag

```
<html>
<head>
<title>Definitions</title>
</head>
<body>
<h2>Definitions for specific word</h2><br />
My nation is <dfn title="Beautiful country">INDIA</dfn>
</body>
</html>
```

Program 3.17
Usage of <acronym> tag

```
<html>
<head>
<title>Acronym</title>
</head>
<body>
<h2>Acronym for specific word</h2><br />
<acronym title="Light Emitting Diode">LED</acronym>
</body>
</html>
```

Program 3.18

Usage of <abbr> tag

```
<html>
<head>
<title>Abbreviation</title>
</head>
<body>
<h2>Abbreviation for specific word</h2><br />
<abbr title="Account">Acc.,</abbr>
</body>
</html>
```

Program 3.19

Usage of <ins>, <del> tag

```
<html>
<head>
<title>Inserted and Deleted Text</title>
</head>
<body>
<ins><u><strong>This text is inserted newly</strong></u></ins><br />
<del><s>This text is deleted from page</s></del><br />
<del><strike>This text is deleted from page</strike></del>
</body>
</html>
```

Program 3.20

Usage of <bdo> tag

```
<html>
<head>
<title>Changing Text Direction</title>
</head>
<body>
<bdo dir="rtl">BACKWORDS</bdo><br />
<bdo dir="ltr">SDROWKCAB</bdo>
</body></html>
```

Program 3.21

Usage of <big>, <small>, <strike> tag

```
<html>
<head>
<title>Changing Text Size</title>
</head>
<body>
<big> Big sized text</big><br />
<small>Small sized text</small><br />
<strike>Strike out text</strike>
</body>
</html>
```

Program 3.22

Usage of <sub>, <sup> tag

```
<html>
<head>
<title>Usage of Sub and Super Script</title>
</head>
<body>
<font size="+1">Water(H<sub></font>2<font size="+1"></sub>O)
contains
Hydrogen (H<sub></font>2<font size="+1"></sub>) and Oxygen (O).<br
/>
I got I<sup></font>st<font size="+1"></sup> Rank</font>
</body></html>
```

Program 3.23

Usage of Unicode Characters

```
<html>
<head>
<title>Unicode Characters</title>
</head>
<body>
a=&trade;<br />
```

```
b=&larr;<br />
c=&uarr;<br />
d=&darr;<br />
e=&rarr;<br />
f=&ge;<br />
g=&le;<br />
h=&oplus;<br />
i=&ne;<br />
j=&sim;<br />
h=&radic;<br />
</body>
</html>
```

Program 3.24

Usage of various colors

```
<html>
<head>
<title>Usage of various color coding</title>
</head>
<body>
<hr color="red"><br />
<hr color="navy"><br />
<hr color="black"><br />
<hr color="blue"><br />
<hr color="green"><br />
<hr color="teal"><br />
<hr color="lime"><br />
<hr color="aqua"><br />
<hr color="maroon"><br />
<hr color="purple"><br />
<hr color="Olive"><br />
<hr color="Gray"><br />
<hr color="silver"><br />
<hr color="yellow"><br />
<hr color="fuchsia"><br />
</body>
</html>
```

- 25 -

Test Program: 3.1

test1.html

```
<html>
<head>
<title>Test page1</title>
</head>
<body>
<h4>Test Page1</h4>
</body>
</html>
```

HTML & CSS

Programming Guide

Chapter 04

Images

04. Images

<img>...</img>

It defines the holding space for the referenced image in the web page.

Attributes:

- src - used to specify the source path.
- border - used to specify the border size.
- width - used to specify the width.
- height - used to specify the height.
- align - used to specify the alignment.
- vspace - used to specify the vertical margin.
- hspace - used to specify the horizontal margin.

Coding Snippets:

Program 4.1

Usage of <body> tag background attribute

```
<html>
<head>
<title>Background Image</title>
</head>
<body background="link/image1.jpg">
<h2>The letters written on the background image</h2>
</body>
</html>
```

Program 4.2

Usage of <img> tag

```
<html>
<head>
<title>Background Image</title>
</head>
<body background="link/image1.jpg">
```

```
<h2>The letters written on the background image</h2>
<img src="link/image2.jpg" border=4 align="center" height=200
width=200>
</body>
</html>
```

Program 4.3

Usage of <img>, <a> tag

```
<html>
<head>
<title>Background Image</title>
</head>
<body background="link/image1.jpg">
<h2>The letters written on the background image</h2>
<a href="link/page1.html"><img src="link/image2.jpg" border=4
align="center" height=200 width=200></a>
</body>
</html>
```

Program 4.4

Usage of <img>, <a> tag

```
<html>
<head>
<title>Background Image</title>
</head>
<body background="link/image1.jpg">
<h2>The letters written on the background image</h2>
<a href="http://www.google.com"><img src="link/image2.jpg" border=4
align="center" height=200 width=200></a>
</body>
</html>
```

Program 4.5

Usage of <img>, <a> tag

```
<html>
```

```
<head>
<title>Background Image</title>
</head>
<body background="link/image1.jpg">
<h2>The letters written on the background image</h2>
<a href="mailto:rvenkatesh@gamil.com"><img src="link/image2.jpg"
border=4 align="center" height=200 width=200></a>
</body>
</html>
```

Program 4.6

Usage of <img>, <a> tag

```
<html>
<head>
<title>Background Image</title>
</head>
<body background="link/image1.jpg">
<h2>The letters written on the background image</h2>
<img src="link/image2.jpg" alt="background image" border=4
align="center" vspace=50 hspace=130 height=200 width=200>
</body>
</html>
```

Program 4.7

Usage of <img> tag with gif animation

```
<html>
<head>
<title>Simple Animation</title>
</head>
<body>
<h3>Simple Animation with GIF File</h3>
<img src="image2.gif" height=300 width=350 border=10>
</body>
</html>
```

Test Program 1:

page1.html

```
<html>
<head>
<title>Test Program 1</title>
</head>
<body>
<h4>Sample Text</h4>
Sample Text 01<br />
Sample Text 02<br />
Sample Text 03<br />
Sample Text 04<br />
Sample Text 05<br />
Sample Text 06<br />
</body>
</html>
```

HTML & CSS

Programming Guide

Chapter 05

Lists

05. Lists

<ol>...</ol>	It defines the ordered list.
<ul>...</ul>	It defines the un-ordered list.
<li>...</li>	It defines the list item. *Attributes:* • type - used to specify the type of the bullets [1, a, A, i, I, disk, circle, square]
<menu>...</menu>	It defines the list/menu of commands. It used for defining the context menus, toolbars and for listing form controls and commands.
<dir>...</dir>	It defines the directory list.
<dl>...</dl>	It defines the description list.
<dd>...</dd>	It defines the term/name in a description list.
<dt>...</dt>	It defines the description of a term/name in a description list.

Coding Snippets:

Program 5.1

Usage of <ol> tag

```
<html>
<head>
<title>Creating Numbered List</title>
</head>
<body>
<h3>My favorite colors</h3>
<ol>
<li>Red</li>
<li>Blue</li>
<li>Green</li>
<li>Black</li>
<li>White</li>
```

```
<li>Purple</li>
<li>Meganda</li>
</ol>
</body>
</html>
```

Program 5.2

Usage of <ol> tag type attributes

```
<html>
<head>
<title>Creating Numbered List</title>
</head>
<body>
<h3>My favorite colors</h3>
<ol>
<li type=A>Red</li>
<li>Blue</li>
<li>Green</li>
<li>Black</li>
<li>White</li>
<li>Purple</li>
<li>Meganda</li>
</ol>
</body>
</html>
```

Program 5.3

Usage of <ul> tag

```
<html>
<head>
<title>Creating Bulleted List</title>
</head>
<body>
<h3>My favorite colors</h3>
<ul>
<li>Red</li>
```

```
<li>Blue</li>
<li>Green</li>
<li>Black</li>
<li>White</li>
<li>Purple</li>
<li>Meganda</li>
</ul>
</body>
</html>
```

Program 5.4
Usage of <ul> tag type attribute

```
<html>
<head>
<title>Creating Bulleted List</title>
</head>
<body>
<h3>My favorite colors</h3>
<ul>
<li type=square>Red</li>
<li type=circle>Blue</li>
<li type=disk>Green</li>
<li type=square>Black</li>
<li type=circle>White</li>
<li type=disk>Purple</li>
</ul>
</body>
</html>
```

Program 5.5
Usage of <ol>, <ul> tag

```
<html>
<head>
<title>Creating Nested List</title>
</head>
<body>
```

```
<h3>My favorite colors</h3>
<ol>
<li>First Choice Colors</li>
<ul>
<li>Red</li>
<li>Blue</li>
<li>Green</li>
</ul>
<br />
<li>Second Choice Colors</li>
<ul>
<li>Black</li>
<li>White</li>
<li>Purple</li>
</ul>
</ol
</body>
</html>
```

Program 5.6

Usage of <dl>, <dt>, <dd> tag

```
<html>
<head>
<title>Creating Definition List</title>
</head>
<body>
<h2>This page contain six test pages
<dl>
<dt>Test Page:1
<dd><a href="test/test1.html">Page1</a>
<dt>Test Page:2
<dd><a href="test/test2.html">Page2</a>
<dt>Test Page:3
<dd><a href="test/test3.html">Page3</a>
<dt>Test Page:4
<dd><a href="test/test4.html">Page4</a>
<dt>Test Page:5
```

```
<dd><a href="test/test5.html">Page5</a>
<dt>Test Page:6
<dd><a href="test/test6.html">Page6</a>
</dl>
</body>
</html>
```

Program 5.7

Usage of <menu> tag

```
<html>
<head>
<title>Creating Menu List</title>
</head>
<body>
<h3>My favorite colors</h3>
<menu>
<li>Red</li>
<li>Blue</li>
<li>Green</li>
<li>Black</li>
<li>White</li>
<li>Purple</li>
<li>Meganda</li>
</menu>
</body>
</html>
```

Program 5.8

Usage of <dir> tag

```
<html>
<head>
<title>Creating Directory List</title>
</head>
<body>
<h3>My favorite colors</h3>
<dir>
```

```
<li>Red</li>
<li>Blue</li>
<li>Green</li>
<li>Black</li>
<li>White</li>
<li>Purple</li>
<li>Meganda</li>
</dir>
</body>
</html>
```

Test Program 5.1

test1.html

```
<html>
<head>
<title>Test page1</title>
</head>
<body>
<h4>Test Page1</h4>
</body>
</html>
```

Test Program 5.2

test2.html

```
<html>
<head>
<title>Test page2</title>
</head>
<body>
<h4>Test Page2</h4>
</body>
</html>
```

Test Program 5.3

test3.html

```
<html>
<head>
<title>Test page3</title>
</head>
<body>
<h4>Test Page3</h4>
</body>
</html>
```

Test Program 5.4

test4.html

```
<html>
<head>
<title>Test page4</title>
</head>
<body>
<h4>Test Page4</h4>
</body>
</html>
```

Test Program 5.5

test5.html

```
<html>
<head>
<title>Test page5</title>
</head>
<body>
<h4>Test Page5</h4>
</body>
</html>
```

Test Program 5.6

test6.html

```
<html>
<head>
<title>Test page6</title>
</head>
<body>
<h4>Test Page6</h4>
</body>
</html>
```

HTML & CSS

Programming Guide

Chapter 06

Links

06. Links

<a>...</a>

It defines the hyperlink text. The hyperlink is a word, group of words, or image that you can click on to jump to another web page.

Attributes:

- href - is used to specify the links destination.
- id - is used to specify the bookmark inside a html document.
- target - is used to specify how to open the web page in the browser.
  _blank: new window; _self: same frame; _parent: parent frame; _top: full body frame; *_framename*: named frame;

By default, links will appear as follows in all browsers:

- An unvisited link is underlined and blue.
- A visited link is underlined and purple.
- An active link is underlined and red.

Coding Snippets:

Program 6.1

Usage of <a> tag for web site linking

```
<html>
<head>
<title>Text Link</title>
</head>
<body>
<a href="http://www.google.com">Click here to visit Google </a>
</body>
</html>
```

Program 6.2
Usage of <a> tag for web site linking

```
<html>
<head>
<title>Image Link</title>
</head>
<body>
<h3>Click the image to visit <u>www.google.com</u></h3>
<a href="http://www. google.com"><img src="link/image1.jpg"</a>
</body>
</html>
```

Program 6.3
Usage of <a> tag for mailing

```
<html>
<head>
<title>Image Link</title>
</head>
<body>
<h3>Click the image to mail to me</h3>
<a href="mailto:rvenkateshieee@gmail.com"><img
src="link/image1.jpg"</a>
</body>
</html>
```

Program 6.4
Usage of <a> tag for mailing

```
<html>
<head>
<title>Text Link</title>
</head>
<body>
<h3>Click here to mail to me:</h3>
<a href="mailto: rvenkateshieee@gmail.com">
rvenkateshieee@gmail.com</a>
```

```
</body>
</html>
```

Program 6.5

Usage of <a> tag for mailing

```
<html>
<head>
<title>Text Link</title>
</head>
<body bgcolor="green" text="#000000" link="red" alink="blue"
vlink="yellow">
<h3>Click here to mail to me:</h3>
<a href="mailto: rvenkateshieee@gmail.com "> rvenkateshieee@gmail.com
</a>
</body>
</html>
```

Program 6.6

Usage of <a> tag for linking with in the page

```
<html>
<head>
<title>Linking with in the page</title>
</head>
<body>
<a name="index"></a>
<dl>
<dt><dd><a href="#target1">Target One</a>
<dt><dd><a href="#target2">Target Two</a>
</dl>
<blockquote>
Target One: Sample Target 01
<br />
Target Two: Sample Target 02
</blockquote>
<a name="target1"></a>
<p>
```

```
<h2>Target One</h2>
Sample Target 01<br />
Sample Target 01<br />
Sample Target 01<br />
Sample Target 01<br />
Sample Target 01<br />
Sample Target 01<br />
Sample Target 01<br />
Sample Target 01<br />
Sample Target 01<br />
Sample Target 01<br />
Sample Target 01<br />
Sample Target 01<br />
Sample Target 01<br />
Sample Target 01<br />
Sample Target 01<br />
</p>
<a href="#index">Back to Index</a>
<a name="target2"></a>
<p>
<h2>Target Two</h2>
Sample Target 02<br />
Sample Target 02<br />
Sample Target 02<br />
Sample Target 02<br />
Sample Target 02<br />
Sample Target 02<br />
Sample Target 02<br />
Sample Target 02<br />
Sample Target 02<br />
Sample Target 02<br />
Sample Target 02<br />
Sample Target 02<br />
Sample Target 02<br />
Sample Target 02<br />
Sample Target 02<br />
Sample Target 02<br />
```

```
</p>
<a href="#index">Back to Index</a>
</body>
</html>
```

HTML & CSS

Programming Guide

Chapter 07

Image Map

07. Image Map

<map>...</map>	It defines an image with clickable areas. *Attributes:* • name - used to specify the name of the imagemap.
<area>...</area>	It defines the clickable areas in the imagemap. *Attributes:* • shape - used to specify the shape of the area. ex: rect, circle • coords - used to specify the co-ordinate points of the shape. [100, 100, 100, 100] • href - used to specify the name of the source file.

Coding Snippets:

Program 7.1

Usage of <map>, <area> tag

```
<html>
<head>
<title>Applying Image Maps</title>
</head>
<body>
<h2>Left Half: About HTML; Right Half: About CSS</h2><br />
<img src="image1.gif" usemap="#imagemap">
<map name="imagemap">
<area shape="rect" coords="0, 0, 250, 360"
href="page1.html">
<area shape="rect" coords="251, 0, 500, 360"
href="page2.html">
</map>
</body>
</html>
```

Program 7.2

Usage of <map>, <area> tag

```
<html>
<head>
<title>Applying Image Maps</title>
</head>
<body>
<h2>Red: About Page 01; Green: About Page 02; Blue: About Page
03</h2><br />
<img src="image1.jpg" usemap="#imagemap">
<map name="imagemap">
<area shape="rect" coords="0, 0, 100, 85" href="page1.html">
<area shape="rect" coords="100, 0, 200, 85" href="page2.html">
<area shape="rect" coords="200, 0, 300, 85" href="page3.html">
</map>
</body>
</html>
```

Program 7.3

Usage of <map>, <area> tag

```
<html>
<head>
<title>Applying Image Maps</title>
</head>
<body>
<h4>Red: Test1; Violet: Test2; Green: Test3; Rose: Test4; Blue: Test5;
Yellow: Test6</h4><br />
<img src="image1.jpg" usemap="#imagemap">
<map name="imagemap">
<area shape="rect" coords="0, 0, 75, 50" href="test1.html">
<area shape="rect" coords="75, 0, 150, 50" href="test2.html">
<area shape="rect" coords="150, 0, 225, 50" href="test3.html">
<area shape="rect" coords="0, 50, 75, 100" href="test4.html">
<area shape="rect" coords="75, 50, 150, 100" href="test5.html">
<area shape="rect" coords="150, 50, 225, 100" href="test6.html">
</map>
```

```
</body>
</html>
```

Program 7.4

Usage of junk method

```
<html>
<head>
<title>Finding Coordinates</title>
</head>
<body>
At the bottom the coordinate points will be displayed, when you move
mouse pointer on the picture.
<a href="junk"><img src="image1.jpg" ismap border=0></a>
</body>
</html>
```

Test Program 7.1

page1.html

```
<html>
<head>
<title>About Page 01</title>
</head>
<body>
<h4>About Page 01</h4>
Sample Text 01<br />
Sample Text 01<br />
Sample Text 01<br />
Sample Text 01<br />
Sample Text 01<br />
Sample Text 01<br />
</body>
</html>
```

Test Program 7.2

page2.html

```
<html>
<head>
<title> About Page 02</title>
</head>
<body>
<h4> About Page 02</h4>
Sample Text 02<br />
Sample Text 02<br />
Sample Text 02<br />
Sample Text 02<br />
Sample Text 02<br />
Sample Text 02<br />
Sample Text 02<br />
Sample Text 02<br />
Sample Text 02<br />
Sample Text 02<br />
</body>
</html>
```

Test Program 7.3

page3.html

```
<html>
<head>
<title> About Page 03</title>
</head>
<body>
<h4> About Page 03</h4>
Sample Text 03<br />
Sample Text 03<br />
Sample Text 03<br />
Sample Text 03<br />
Sample Text 03<br />
Sample Text 03<br />
Sample Text 03<br />
Sample Text 03<br />
Sample Text 03<br />
</body>
</html>
```

HTML & CSS

Programming Guide

Chapter 08

Tables

08. Tables

<table>...</table>	It defines the tables. The table is divided into rows and each row is divided into data cells. *Attributes:* • align - used to specify the alignment. • background - used to provide the background image. • bgcolor - used to specify the background color. • border - used to specify the border width. • cellpadding - used to specify the pixels for cellpadding. • cellspacing - used to specify the pixels for cellspacing. • height - used to specify the height of table. • width - used to specify the width of table.
<tr>...</tr>	It defines the row of the table. *Attributes:* • align - used to specify the alignment. • bgcolor - used to specify the background color. • height - used to specify the height of row. • width - used to specify the width of row. • rowspan - used to combine to two row cells. • valign - used to specify the vertical alignment.
<td>...</td>	It defines the data cells of the table. *Attributes:* • align - used to specify the alignment. • bgcolor - used to specify the background color. • height - used to specify the height of cell. • width - used to specify the width of cell. • rowspan - used to combine to two row cells. • valign - used to specify the vertical alignment.

<thead>...</thead>	It defines the table header section.
<tfoot>...</tfoot>	It defines the table footer section.

Coding Snippets:

Program 8.1

Usage of <table>, <tr>, <td> tags

```
<html>
<head>
<title>Simple Table</title>
</head>
<body>
<table width="50%" border="1">
<tr>
<td>cell row1 col1</td>
<td>cell row1 col2</td>
</tr>
<tr>
<td>cell row2 col1</td>
<td>cell row2 col2</td>
</tr>
</table>
</body>
</html>
```

Program 8.2

Usage of <table>, <td>, <tr> with its attributes

```
<html>
<head>
<title>Simple Table</title>
</head>
<body>
<table width="50%" height="100" border="1">
<tr>
<td align="left" valign="top">top left</td>
```

```
<td align="right" valign="top">top right</td>
</tr>
<tr>
<td align="left" valign="bottom">bottom left</td>
<td align="right" valign="bottom">bottom right</td>
</tr>
</table>
</body>
</html>
```

Program 8.3

Inserting image into the table

```
<html>
<head>
<title>Table with image</title>
</head>
<body>
<table border="10">
<tr>
<td><img src="image1.jpg"></td>
</tr>
</table>
</body>
</html>
```

Program 8.4

Changing the width of table cells

```
<html>
<head>
<title>Simple Table</title>
</head>
<body>
<table width="400" height="100" border="1">
<tr>
<td width="140">top left</td>
<td width="260">top right</td>
```

```
</tr>
<tr>
<td>bottom left</td>
<td>bottom right</td>
</tr>
</table>
</body>
</html>
```

Program 8.5

Changing the width of the table cells

```
<html>
<head>
<title>Simple Table</title>
</head>
<body>
<table width="400" height="100" border="1">
<tr>
<td width="35%">top left</td>
<td width="65%">top right</td>
</tr>
<tr>
<td>bottom left</td>
<td>bottom right</td>
</tr>
</table>
</body>
</html>
```

Program 8.6

Creating empty cells in table

```
<html>
<head>
<title>Simple Table</title>
</head>
<body>
```

```
<table width="400" height="100" border="1">
<tr>
<td width="35%">top left</td>
<td width="65%"> </td>
</tr>
<tr>
<td>bottom left</td>
<td> </td>
</tr>
</table>
</body>
</html>
```

Program 8.7

Usage of cell padding effect

```
<html>
<head>
<title>Cell Padding</title>
</head>
<body>
Cell Padding Effect: <br /><br />
<table border="3" cellpadding="20">
<tr>
<td>top left</td>
<td>top right</td>
</tr>
<tr>
<td>bottom left</td>
<td>bottom right</td>
</tr>
</table>
</body>
</html>
```

Program 8.8

Usage of Cell Spacing effect

```
<html>
<head>
<title>Cell Spacing</title>
</head>
<body>
Cell Spacing Effect: <br /><br />
<table border="3" cellspacing="10">
<tr>
<td>top left</td>
<td>top right</td>
</tr>
<tr>
<td>bottom left</td>
<td>bottom right</td>
</tr>
</table>
</body>
</html>
```

Program 8.9

Creating tables with different color

```
<html>
<head>
<title>Table with background Color</title>
</head>
<body>
<table width="300" bgcolor="#66ccff" border="3">
<tr>
<td>top left</td>
<td>top right</td>
</tr>
<tr>
<td>bottom left</td>
<td>bottom right</td>
```

```
</tr>
</table>
</body>
</html>
```

Program 8.10

Creating table cells with different colors

```
<html>
<head>
<title>Table with background Color</title>
</head>
<body>
<table width="300" border="2">
<tr bgcolor="blue">
<td>top left</td>
<td>top right</td>
</tr>
<tr bgcolor="green">
<td>bottom left</td>
<td>bottom right</td>
</tr>
</table>
</body>
</html>
```

Program 8.11

Creating table cells with different colors

```
<html>
<head>
<title>Table with background Color</title>
</head>
<body>
<table width="300" border="2">
<caption> Colorful Table </caption>
<tr bgcolor="blue">
<td>top left</td>
```

```
<td>top right</td>
</tr>
<tr bgcolor="green">
<td bgcolor="green">bottom left</td>
<td bgcolor="red">bottom right</td>
</tr>
</table>
</body>
</html>
```

Program 8.12

Creating Column Span Effect

```
<html>
<head>
<title>Column span</title>
</head>
<body>
<table width="40%" border="1">
<tr>
<td colspan="2">a</td>
<td>b</td>
</tr>
<tr>
<td>a</td>
<td>b</td>
<td>c</td>
</tr>
</table>
</body>
</html>
```

Program 8.13

Creating Row Span Effect

```
<html>
<head>
<title>Row span</title>
```

```
</head>
<body>
<table width="40%" border="1">
<tr>
<td rowspan="2">a</td>
<td>b</td>
<td>c</td>
</tr>
<tr>
<td>d</td>
<td>e</td>
</tr>
</table>
</body>
</html>
```

Program 8.14

Creating nested tables

```
<html>
<head>
<title>Nesting of Table</title>
</head>
<body>
<table width="750" border="0">
<tr>
<td width="25%"> </td>
<td width="25%"> </td>
<td width="25%"> </td>
<table border="2" width="100%">
<tr>
<td width="50%">1-</td>
<td width="50%">HTML</td>
</tr>
<tr>
<td width="50%">2-</td>
<td width="50%">BASIC</td>
</tr>
```

```
<tr>
<td width="50%">3-</td>
<td width="50%">FORTRON</td>
</tr>
</table>
</td>
<td width="25%"> </td>
</tr>
</table>
</body>
</html>
```

HTML & CSS

Programming Guide

Chapter 09

Audio

09. Audio

<bgsound>...</bgsound>	It defines the background music file for the web page. *Attributes:* • src - used to specify the source path of the sound file.
<embed>...</embed>	It is used to embed sound file into the web page. *Attributes:* • src - used to specify the source file path & name. • type - used to specify the type of file. [audio/wav, audio/aiff] • width - used to specify the width of the player size. • height - used to specify the height of the player size.
<object>...</object>	It is used to define sound file into the web page. *Attributes:* • data - used to specify the source file name. • type - used to specify the type of sound file. [audio/wav, audio/aiff] • width - used to specify the width of the player size. • height - used to specify the height of the player size.
<param>...</param>	It defines the parameters for object tag. *Attributes:* • name - used to specify the name of the parameter. • value - used to specify the value for the parameter.

Coding Snippets:

Program 9.1

Usage of <bgsound> tag

```
<html>
<head>
<title>Adding Sound File</title>
</head>
<body>
Here is the sound file:
<br />
<bgsound src="sound1.wav">
</body>
</html>
```

Program 9.2

Usage of <embed> tag

```
<html>
<head>
<title>Adding Sound File</title>
</head>
<body>
Here is the sound file:
<br />
<embed src="sound1.wav" type="audio/wav" width="145" height="60">
</body>
</html>
```

Program 9.3

Creating downloadable sound file

```
<html>
<head>
<title>Adding Sound File</title>
</head>
<body>
```

Here is the sound file:
```
<br />
<a href="sound1.wav">Get the sound file here</a><br />
<bgsound src="sound1.wav">
</body>
</html>
```

Program 9.4

Usage of <object>, <param> tag

```
<html>
<head>
<title>Adding Sound File</title>
</head>
<body>
Here is the sound file:
<br />
<object data="sound1.wav" type="audio/wav" width="145" height="60">
<param name="autostart" value="true">
</object>
</body>
</html>
```

Program 9.5

Usage of <noembed> tag

```
<html>
<head>
<title>Adding Sound File</title>
</head>
<body>
Here is the sound file:
<br />
<object data="sound1.wav" type="audio/wav" width="145" height="60">
<param name="autostart" value="true">
<embed src="sound1.wav" type="audio/wav" width="145" height="60">
<noembed>
<a href="sound1.wav">Get the sound file here</a><br />
```

```
<noembed>
</object>
<bgsound src="sound1.wav">
</body>
</html>
```

HTML & CSS

Programming Guide

Chapter 10

Video

10. Video

<img>...</img>	It defines the moving dynamic frames for the web page. *Attributes:* • dynsrc - used to specify the name of the movie file. • width - used to specify the width of the movie. • height - used to specify the height of the movie.
<embed>...</embed>	It is used to embed movie file in the web page. *Attributes:* • src - used to specify the source file path & name. • width - used to specify the width of the player size. • height - used to specify the height of the player size.
<object>...</object>	It is used to define movie file in the web page. *Attributes:* • data - used to specify the source file name. • width - used to specify the width of the player size. • height - used to specify the height of the player size.
<param>...</param>	It defines the parameters for object tag. *Attributes:* • name - used to specify the name of the parameter. • value - used to specify the value for the parameter.

Coding Snippets:

Program 10.1

Usage of <img> tag

```
<html>
<head>
<title>Adding Movie File</title>
</head>
<body>
Here is the movie file:
<br />
<img dynsrc="movie1.mpg" width="300" height="200">
</body>
</html>
```

Program 10.2

Usage of <embed> tag

```
<html>
<head>
<title>Adding Movie File</title>
</head>
<body>
Here is the movie file:
<br />
<embed src="movie1.mpg" width="300" height="200">
</body>
</html>
```

Program 10.3

Usage of <object>, <param> tag

```
<html>
<head>
<title>Adding Movie File</title>
</head>
<body>
```

Here is the movie file:

<object data="movie1.mpg" width="300" height="200">
<param name="autostart" value="true">
</body>
</html>

Program 10.4
Creating downloadable movie file

```
<html>
<head>
<title>Adding Movie File</title>
</head>
<body>
Here is the movie file:
<br />
<a href="movie1.mpg">Get the movie here</a><br />
<img dynsrc="movie1.mpg" width="300" height="200">
</body>
</html>
```

Program 10.5
Usage of <noembed> tag

```
<html>
<head>
<title>Adding Movie File</title>
</head>
<body>
Here is the movie file:
<br />
<!--
<object data="movie1.mpg" width="300" height="200">
<param name="autostart" value="true">
<embed src="movie1.mpg" width="300" height="200">
//-->
<noembed>
```

```
<a href="movie1.mpg">Get the movie here</a><br />
<noembed>
</object>
<img dynsrc="movie1.mpg" width="300" height="200">
</body>
</html>
```

HTML & CSS

Programming Guide

Chapter 11

Flash Animations

11. Flash Animations

<object>...</object>	It is used to define flash file in the web page. *Attributes:* • classid - used to specify the id of the Active X control. • codebase - used to specify the URL address for Active X control. • width - used to specify the width of flash movie. • height - used to specify the height of flash movie.
<param>...</param>	It defines the parameters for object tag. *Attributes:* • name - used to specify the name of the parameter. • value - used to specify the value for the parameter.

Coding Snippets:

Program 11.1
Creating flash embedded web page

```
<html>
<head>
<title>
Flash Creation
</title>
<body>
<object classid="clsid:D27CDB6E-AE6D-11cf-96B8-444553540000"
codebase="http://download.macromedia.com/pub/shockwave/cabs/flash/swflash.cab#version=5,0,2,0"
width="500" height="250">
<param name="src" value="worldmap.swf">
<param name="quality" value="high">
```

```
</object>
</body>
</html>
```

Program 11.2

Creating flash embedded web page

```
<html>
<head>
<title>
Flash Creation
</title>
<body>
<object classid="clsid:D27CDB6E-AE6D-11cf-96B8-444553540000"
codebase="http://download.macromedia.com/pub/shockwave/cabs/flas
h/swflash.cab#version=5,0,2,0"
width="500"
height="250">
<param name="src" value="flash2.swf">
<param name="quality" value="high">
</object>
</body>
</html>
```

HTML & CSS

Programming Guide

Chapter 12

Interactive Forms

12. Interactive Forms

<form>...</form>	It defines the input forms in the web page. *Attributes:* • method - used to specify the method types (Post/Get). • action - used to specify source file for storing form entries.
<input>...</input>	It defines the input field types of the form. *Attributes:* • type - used to specify the type of input field. • text - used to provide text field control. • radio - used to provide radio button control. • checkbox - used to provide checkbox control. • password - used to provide password text field control. • submit - used to provide submit button. • file - used to provide file browsing control. • reset - used to provide reset button. • name - used to specify the name of the control. • value - used to provide values to the control.
<select>...</select>	It defines the selection list control. *Attributes:* • name - used to provide the name to the control. • multiple - used to specify the multiple list control.
<option>...</option>	It defines the option lists for selection control. *Attributes:* • value - used to provide the value to the particular list option.
<textarea>...</textarea>	It defines the text area field control for multiline input.

Attributes:

- name - used to specify the name of the control.
- rows - used to specify the number of rows in the text area filed.
- cols - used to specify the number of columns in the text area field.

Coding Snippets:

Program 12.1

Usage of <form>, <input> tag with text field

```
<html>
<head>
<title>Adding Form Controls</title>
</head>
<body bgcolor="#ffffff">
Where do you want to go on vacation:
<hr>
<form method="post" action="/cgi-bin/test.cgi">
<b>Name:</b>
<input type="text" name="place_name">
<br />
<b>Date:</b>
<input type="text" name="Date">
</form>
</body>
</html>
```

Program 12.2

Usage of <form>, <input> tag with password field

```
<html>
<head>
<title>Adding Form Controls</title>
</head>
<body bgcolor="#ffffff">
Enter your Name and Pass Word:
<hr>
<form method="post" action="/cgi-bin/test.cgi">
<b>Name         :</b>
<input type="text" name="place_name">
<br />
<b>Pass Word:</b>
<input type="password" name="pswd">
</form>
</body>
</html>
```

Program 12.3

Usage of <form>, <input> tag with radio button

```
<html>
<head>
<title>Adding Form Controls</title>
</head>
<body bgcolor="#ffffff">
Where do you want to go on vacation:
<hr>
<form method="post" action="/cgi-bin/test.cgi">
<input type="radio" name="vacation" value="Aruba" checked>Aruba<br
/>
```

```
<input type="radio" name="vacation" value="Paris" >Paris<br />
<input type="radio" name="vacation" value="Canada" >Canana<br />
<input type="radio" name="vacation" value="Houston" >Houston<br />
</form>
</body>
</html>
```

Program 12.4

Usage of <form>, <input> tag with check boxes

```
<html>
<head>
<title>Adding Form Controls</title>
</head>
<body bgcolor="#ffffff">
Where do you want to go on vacation:
<hr>
<form method="post" action="/cgi-bin/test.cgi">
<input type="checkbox" name="vacation" value="Aruba"
checked>Aruba<br />
<input type="checkbox" name="vacation" value="Paris" >Paris<br />
<input type="checkbox" name="vacation" value="Canada" >Canana<br />
<input type="checkbox" name="vacation" value="Houston" >Houston<br
/>
</form>
</body>
</html>
```

Program 12.5

Usage of <form>, <select> tag with selection list

```
<html>
<head>
```

```
<title>Adding Form Controls</title>
</head>
<body bgcolor="#ffffff">
Please Select an appliance type:
<br />
<form method="post" action="/cgi-bin/test.cgi">
<select name="appliance">
<option>Television</option>
<option>Bridge</option>
<option>Radio</option>
<option>Grinder</option>
<option>Mixie</option>
<option>Iron Box</option>
</select>
</form>
</body>
</html>
```

Program 12.6

Usage of <form>, <select> with multiple selection list

```
<html>
<head>
<title>Adding Form Controls</title>
</head>
<body bgcolor="#ffffff">
What are your favorite colors:
<br />
<form method="post" action="/cgi-bin/test.cgi">
<select name="color" multiple size="5">
<option>Red</option>
<option>Green</option>
<option>Blue</option>
```

```
<option>Orange</option>
<option>Yellow</option>
<option>Brown</option>
<option>White</option>
<option>Black</option>
</select>
</form>
</body>
</html>
```

Program 12.7

Usage of <form>, <textarea> tag

```
<html>
<head>
<title>Adding Form Controls</title>
</head>
<body bgcolor="#ffffff">
Enter your comments:
<br />
<form method="post" action="/cgi-bin/test.cgi">
<textarea name="mytext" rows="10" cols="10">Replace this text with your
own.</textarea>
</form>
</body>
</html>
```

Program 12.8

Usage of <form>, <input> tag with submit and reset button

```
<html>
<head>
<title>Adding Form Controls</title>
```

```
</head>
<body bgcolor="#ffffff">
Where do you want to go on vacation:
<hr>
<form method="post" action="/cgi-bin/test.cgi">
<input type="radio" name="vacation" value="Aruba" checked>Aruba<br />
<input type="radio" name="vacation" value="Paris" >Paris<br />
<input type="radio" name="vacation" value="Canada" >Canana<br />
<input type="radio" name="vacation" value="Houston" >Houston<br />
<br /><br />
<input type="submit" value="Submit form">
<input type="reset" value="Reset form">
</form>
</body>
</html>
```

Program 12.9

Usage of <form>, <input> tag with file browsing

```
<html>
<head>
<title>Adding Form Controls</title>
</head>
<body bgcolor="#ffffff">
Put this file on the server:
<form method="post" action="/cgi-bin/test.cgi">
<input type="file" name="myfile">
<input type="submit" value="Send File">
</form>
</body>
</html>
```

Program 12.10

Usage of all <form> related tags

```
<html>
<head>
<title>Adding Form Controls</title>
</head>
<body bgcolor="#ffffff">
<font size=+1>My company feedback form</font>
<hr>
<form method="post" action="/cgi-bin/test.cgi">
<table width=100%>
<tr><td>
<b>Name:</b>
<input type="text" name=employee_name">
</td>
<td>
<b>Department:</b>
<input type="radio" name="dept" value="Sales">Sales
<input type="radio" name="dept" value="HR">HR
<input type="radio" name="dept" value="PR">PR
<input type="radio" name="dept" value="R&D">R&D
</td>
</tr>
<tr>
<td>
<b>Which internet sites have you visited:</b><br />
<input type="checkbox" name="sites" value="company" checked>My
company's Web site<br />
<input type="checkbox" name="sites" value="Excite">Excite search
engine<br />
<input type="checkbox" name="sites" value="Lycos">Lycos search
engine<br />
```

```
<input type="checkbox" name="sites" value="CNN">CNN Cable news<br
/>
<input type="checkbox" name="sites" value="ESPN">ESPN Sports<br />
<input type="checkbox" name="sites" value="Dow Jones">Dow Johns
Report<br />
<input type="checkbox" name="sites" value="WSJ">Wall Street Journel
</td>
<td valign=top>
<br />
<b>Comments:</b><br />
<textarea name="comments" cols="30" rows="7"></textarea>
</td></tr>
</table>
<p>
<input type="submit" value="Submit Form">
<input type="reset" value="Reset Form">
</form>
</body>
</html>
```

Program 12.11

Usage of all <form> related tags

```
<html>
<head>
<title>Adding Form Controls</title>
</head>
<body bgcolor="#ffffff">
Where do you want to go on vacation:
<hr>
<form method="post" action="form10.html">
<input type="radio" name="vacation" value="Aruba" checked>Aruba<br
/>
```

```
<input type="radio" name="vacation" value="Paris" >Paris<br />
<input type="radio" name="vacation" value="Canada" >Canana<br />
<input type="radio" name="vacation" value="Houston" >Houston<br />
<br /><br />
<input type="submit" value="Submit form">
<input type="reset" value="Reset form">
</form>
</body>
</html>
```

HTML & CSS

Programming Guide

Chapter 13

Frames

13. Frames

<frame>...</frame>	It defines the frame segment of the web page. *Attributes:* • src - used to specify the name of the source file for the frame. • name - used to specify the name of the frame.
<frameset>...</frameset>	It defines the frameset of frame segment of the web page. *Attributes:* • rows - used to specify the row fragment. • cols - used to specify the column fragment.
<base>	It defines the base target for all relative URLs in a web page. *Attributes:* • href - used to specify the base url for all relative urls in a web page. • target - used to specify the target frame name [any_window, _parent, _top, _blank, _self, a_window]

Coding Snippets:

13.1 Normal Frames

Program 13.1.1
Usage of <frame> tag

```
<html>
<head>
<title> Simple Frames </title>
</head>
<frameset cols="15%,85%">
<frame src="test1.html">
<frame src="test2.html">
```

```
</frameset>
</html>
```

Program 13.1.2
Usage of <frame> tag

```
<html>
<head>
<title> Simple Frames </title>
</head>
<frameset cols="*,2*">
<frame src="test1.html">
<frame src="test2.html">
</frameset>
</html>
```

Program 13.1.3
Usage of <frame> tag

```
<html>
<head>
<title> Simple Frames </title>
</head>
<frameset cols="50%,50%">
<frame src="test1.html">
<frame src="test2.html">
<noframe>
<head>
<title>Your Home Page</title>
</head>
<body>
This navigator does not support frames
</body>
</html>
</noframe>
</frameset>
</html>
```

Program 13.1.4

Usage of <frame> tag

```
<html>
<head>
<title> Simple Frames </title>
</head>
<frameset rows="50%,50%" cols="*,*,*">
<frame src="test1.html">
<frame src="test2.html">
<frame src="test3.html">
<frame src="test4.html">
<frame src="test5.html">
<frame src="test6.html">
</frameset>
</html>
```

Program 13.1.5

Usage of <frame> tag

```
<html>
<head>
<title> Simple Frames </title>
</head>
<frameset cols="*,*">
<frame src="test1.html">
<frame scrolling="YES" noresize marginwidth="50" marginheight="50"
src="test2.html">
</frameset>
</html>
```

Program 13.1.6

Usage of <frame> tag

```
<html>
<head>
<title> Simple Frames </title>
</head>
```

```
<frameset rows="50%,50%" cols="*,*,*" frameborder="0">
<frame src="test1.html">
<frame src="test2.html">
<frame src="test3.html">
<frame src="test4.html">
<frame src="test5.html">
<frame src="test6.html">
</frameset>
</html>
```

Program 13.1.7

Usage of <frame> tag

```
<html>
<head>
<title> Simple Frames </title>
</head>
<frameset rows="20%,80%">
<frame src="test1.html">
<frameset cols="20%,80%">
<frame src="test2.html">
<frame src="test3.html">
</frameset>
</frameset>
</html>
```

Program 13.1.8

Usage of <frame> tag

```
<html>
<head>
<title> Simple Frames </title>
</head>
<frameset rows="30%,70%">
<frameset cols="20%,80%">
<frame src="test1.html">
<frame src="test2.html">
</frameset>
```

```
<frameset cols="40%,60%">
<frame src="test3.html">
<frame src="test4.html">
</frameset>
</frameset>
</html>
```

Program 13.1.9

Usage of <frame> tag

```
<html>
<head>
<title> Simple Frames </title>
</head>
<frameset rows="15%,70%,15%">
<frame src="test1.html" noresize>
<frameset cols="20%,80%">
<frame src="test2.html">
<frame src="test3.html">
</frameset>
<frame src="test4.html">
</frameset>
</html>
```

Program 13.1.10

Usage of <frame> tag

```
<html>
<head>
<title> Simple Frames </title>
</head>
<frameset rows="15%,65%,20%">
<frame src="test1.html">
<frame src="test2.html">
<frame src="test3.html">
</frameset>
</html>
```

Program 13.1.11

Usage of <frame> tag

```
<html>
<head>
<title> Simple Frames </title>
</head>
<frameset cols="20%,80%">
<frame src="test1.html">
<frameset rows="30%,70%">
<frame src="test2.html">
<frame src="test3.html">
</frameset>
</frameset>
</html>
```

Test Program 13.1.1

test1.html

```
<html>
<head>
<title>Test page1</title>
</head>
<body>
<h4>Test Page1</h4>
</body>
</html>
```

Test Program 13.1.2

test2.html

```
<html>
<head>
<title>Test page2</title>
</head>
<body>
<h4>Test Page2</h4>
</body></html>
```

Test Program 13.1.3

test3.html

```
<html>
<head>
<title>Test page3</title>
</head>
<body>
<h4>Test Page3</h4>
</body>
</html>
```

Test Program 13.1.4

test4.html

```
<html>
<head>
<title>Test page4</title>
</head>
<body>
<h4>Test Page4</h4>
</body>
</html>
```

Test Program 13.1.5

test5.html

```
<html>
<head>
<title>Test page5</title>
</head>
<body>
<h4>Test Page5</h4>
</body>
</html>
```

Test Program 13.1.6

test6.html

```
<html>
<head>
<title>Test page6</title>
</head>
<body>
<h4>Test Page6</h4>
</body>
</html>
```

13.2 Navigational Frames

Program 13.2.1

Usage of navigating frame techniques

```
<html>
<head>
<title> Navigational Frames </title>
</head>
<frameset cols="50%,50%">
<frame src="test1.html">
<frame src="test2.html">
</frameset>
</html>
```

test1.html

```
<html>
<head>
<title>Test page1</title>
</head>
<body>
<h4>This is the page: 1</h4>
<a href="page1.html">About Page_01</a>
</body>
</html>
```

test2.html

```
<html>
<head>
<title>Test page2</title>
</head>
<body>
<h4>This is the page: 2</h4>
<a href="page2.html">About Page_02</a>
</body>
</html>
```

Program 13.2.2

Usage of navigational frame techniques

```
<html>
<head>
<title> Simple Frames </title>
</head>
<frameset cols="50%,50%">
<frame src="test1.html" name="left">
<frame src="page1.html" name="right">
</frameset>
</html>
```

test1.html

```
<html>
<head>
<title>Test page1</title>
</head>
<body>
<br />
<a href="page1.html" target="right">About Page_01</a>
<br />
<a href="page2.html" target="right">About Page_02</a>
<br />
<a href="page3.html" target="right">About Page_03</a>
```

```
<br />
</body>
</html>
```

Program 13.2.3

Usage of navigational frame techniques

```
<html>
<head>
<title> Navigational Frames </title>
</head>
<frameset cols="50%,50%">
<frame src="test1.html" name="left">
<frame src="page1.html" name="right">
</frameset>
</html>
```

test1.html

```
<html>
<head>
<title>Test page1</title>
<base target="right">
</head>
<body>
<br />
<a href="page1.html" >About Page_01</a>
<br />
<a href="page2.html" >About Page_02</a>
<br />
<a href="page3.html" >About Page_03</a>
<br />
</body>
</html>
```

Program 13.2.4

Usage of navigational frame techniques

```
<html>
<head>
<title> Navigational Frames </title>
</head>
<h1>Load in New Windows</h1>
<br />
<br />
<h2><a href="page1.html" target="any_window">About Page_01</a><br
/> </h2>
<h2><a href="page2.html" target="any_window">About Page_02</a><br
/></h2>
<h2><a href="page3.html" target="any_window">About Page_03</a><br
/></h2>
</body>
</html>
```

Program 13.2.5

Usage of navigational frame techniques

```
<html>
<head>
<title> Navigational Frames </title>
</head>
<h1>Load in New Windows</h1>
<br />
<br />
<h2><a href="page1.html" target="_blank">About Page_01</a><br />
</h2>
<h2><a href="page2.html" target="_blank">About Page_02</a><br
/></h2>
<h2><a href="page3.html" target="_blank">About Page_03</a><br
/></h2>
</body>
</html>
```

Program 13.2.6

Usage of navigational frame techniques

```
<html>
<head>
<title> Navigational Frames </title>
</head>
<h1>Load in New Windows</h1>
<br />
<br />
<h2><a href="page1.html" target="_self">About Page_01</a><br />
</h2>
<h2><a href="page2.html" target="_self">About Page_02</a><br /></h2>
<h2><a href="page3.html" target="_self">About Page_03</a><br /></h2>
</body>
</html>
```

Program 13.2.7

Usage of navigational frame techniques

```
<html>
<head>
<title> Navigational Frames </title>
</head>
<h1>Load in New Windows</h1>
<br />
<br />
<h2><a href="page1.html" target="_parent">About Page_01</a><br />
</h2>
<h2><a href="page2.html" target="_parent">About Page_02</a><br
/></h2>
<h2><a href="page3.html" target="_parent">About Page_03</a><br
/></h2>
</body>
</html>
```

Program 13.2.8

Usage of navigational frame techniques

```
<html>
<head>
<title> Navigational Frames </title>
</head>
<h1>Load in New Windows</h1>
<br />
<br />
<h2><a href="page1.html" target="_top">About Page_01</a><br />
</h2>
<h2><a href="page2.html" target="_top">About Page_02</a><br /></h2>
<h2><a href="page3.html" target="_top">About Page_03</a><br /></h2>
</body>
</html>
```

Program 13.2.9

Usage of navigational frame techniques

```
<html>
<head>
<title> Navigational Frames </title>
<base target="a_window">
</head>
<h1>Load in New Windows</h1>
<br />
<br />
<h2><a href="page1.html" >About Page_01</a><br /> </h2>
<h2><a href="page2.html" >About Page_02</a><br /></h2>
<h2><a href="page3.html" >About Page_03</a><br /></h2>
</body>
</html>
```

Program 13.2.10

Usage of navigational frame techniques

```
<html>
<head>
<title> Navigational Frames </title>
<base target="a_window">
</head>
<br />
<a href="page1.html" >About Page_01</a><br />
<a href="page2.html" >About Page_02</a><br />
<a href="page3.html" >About Page_03</a><br />
<a href="page1.html" >About Page_01</a><br />
<a href="page2.html" >About Page_02</a><br />
<a href="page3.html" >About Page_03</a><br />
<a href="page1.html" >About Page_01</a><br />
<a href="page2.html" >About Page_02</a><br />
<a href="page3.html" >About Page_03</a><br />
<a href="page1.html" >About Page_01</a><br />
<a href="page2.html" >About Page_02</a><br />
<a href="page3.html" >About Page_03</a><br />
</body>
</html>
```

Test Program 13.2.1

page1.html

```
<html>
<head>
<title>Test Page Content 01</title>
</head>
<body>
<h4>About Page_01</h4>
Sample Text Page_01<br />
Sample Text Page_01<br />
Sample Text Page_01<br />
Sample Text Page_01<br />
Sample Text Page_01<br />
```

```
Sample Text Page_01<br />
</body>
</html>
```

Test Program 13.2.2

page2.html

```
<html>
<head>
<title>Test Page Content 02</title>
</head>
<body>
<h4>About Page_02</h4>
Sample Text Page_02<br />
Sample Text Page_02<br />
Sample Text Page_02<br />
Sample Text Page_02<br />
Sample Text Page_02<br />
Sample Text Page_02<br />
</body>
</html>
```

Test Program 13.2.3

page3.html

```
<html>
<head>
<title>Test Page Content 03</title>
</head>
<body>
<h4>About Page_03</h4>
Sample Text Page_03<br />
Sample Text Page_03<br />
Sample Text Page_03<br />
Sample Text Page_03<br />
Sample Text Page_03<br />
Sample Text Page_03<br />
</body></html>
```

HTML & CSS

Programming Guide

Chapter 14

Layers

14. Layers

<layer>...</layer>	It defines the layer segment in the web page with absolute positioning. *Attributes:* • background - used to specify background image. • bgcolor - used to specify background color. • src - used to specify source file name. • left - used to specify the pixels from the left corner of window. • top - used to specify the pixels from the top corner of window. • height - used to specify height of the layer. • width - used to specify width of the layer. • z-index - used to specify the pixels in z coordinates. • pagex - used to specify the pixels with reference to window x axis. • pagey - used to specify the pixels with reference to window y axis.
<ilayer>...</ilayer>	It defines the layer segment in the web page with relative positioning.
<nolayer>...</nolayer>	It is used in the browsers which does not support layers.

Coding Snippets:

Program 14.1
Usage of <layer> tag

```
<html>
<head>
<title>A Simple Layer</title>
</head>
```

```
<layer top="70" left="70">
Kannan <br />
Mahesh <br />
Nandhini <br />
</layer>
</html>
```

Program 14.2

Usage of <layer> tag

```
<html>
<head>
<title>A Simple Layer</title>
</head>
<layer top="70" left="70" bgcolor="red">
Kannan <br />
Mahesh <br />
Nandhini <br />
</layer>
</html>
```

Program 14.3

Usage of <layer> tag

```
<html>
<head>
<title>A Simple Layer</title>
</head>
<layer top="70" left="70" background="image1.jpg">
Kannan <br />
Mahesh <br />
Nandhini <br />
</layer>
</html>
```

Program 14.4

Usage of <layer> tag

```
<html>
<head>
<title>A Simple Layer</title>
</head>
<layer top="70" left="70" background="image1.jpg" height="100"
width="100">
Kannan <br />
Mahesh <br />
Nandhini <br />
</layer>
</html>
```

Program 14.5

Usage of<layer> tag

```
<html>
<head>
<title>A Simple Layer</title>
</head>
<layer top="70" left="70" background="image1.jpg" height="100"
width="100" src="test.html">
</layer>
</html>
```

Program 14.6

Usage of multiple layers

```
<html>
<head>
<title>A Simple Layer</title>
</head>
<layer left=25 top=48>
<img src="image1.jpg" width="200" height="180" border="0">
</layer>
<layer left=35 top=98>
```

```
<img src="image2.jpg" width="210" height="117" border="0">
</layer>
</html>
```

Program 14.7

Usage of nested layers

```
<html>
<head>
<title>A Simple Layer</title>
</head>
<layer left=25 top=48>
<img src="image1.jpg" width="200" height="180" border="0" >
<layer left=35 top=98 z-index="40">
<img src="image2.jpg" width="210" height="117" border="0" >
</layer>
</layer>
</html>
```

Program 14.8

Usage of nested layers

```
<html>
<head>
<title>A Simple Layer</title>
</head>
<layer left=25 top=48>
<img src="image1.jpg" width="200" height="180" border="0" >
<layer left=35 top=98 z-index="40" visibility=HIDE>
<img src="image2.jpg" width="210" height="117" border="0" >
</layer>
</layer>
</html>
```

Program 14.9

Usage of pagex, pagey attributes

```
<html>
<head>
<title>A Simple Layer</title>
</head>
<layer left=25 top=48>
<img src="image1.jpg" width="200" height="180" border="0" >
<layer pagex="250" pagey="250">
<img src="image2.jpg" width="210" height="117" border="0" >
</layer>
</layer>
</html>
```

Program 14.10

Usage of <ilayer> tag

```
<html>
<head>
<title>An Inline Layer</title>
</head>
<layer top=25 left=45>
<img src="image1.jpg" width=222 height=136 border=0>
</layer>
<ilayer top="28" left="100">
<h2>Heading positioned relative to the first layer, not the upper left of
the browser window</h2>
</ilayer>
</html>
```

Program 14.11

Usage of <nolayer> tag

```
<html>
<head>
<title>An Inline Layer</title>
</head>
```

```
<layer top=25 left=45>
<img src="image1.jpg" width=400 height=300 border=0>
</layer>
<ilayer top="28" left="100">
<h2>Heading positioned relative to the first layer, not the upper left of
the browser window</h2>
</ilayer>
<nolayer>
<body bgcolor="#ffffff">
<H1>You are not using Netscape Navigator...!<h1>
</nolayer>
</html>
```

HTML & CSS

Programming Guide

Chapter 15

Scripting

15. Scripting

`<script>...</script>`	It is used define the client side script, such as javascript, vbscript. *Values:* • src - used to provide the path of external script file. • type - used to provide the MIME type of the script. text/javascript; text/vbscript; application/ecmascript; application/javascript; text/vbscript;
`<noscript>...</noscript>`	It defines the alternate content for scripting non-supporting browsers.

Coding Snippets:

Program 15.1
Usage of <script> tag

```
<html>
<head>
<title>Usage of script tag.</title>
</head>
<body>
<script type="text/javascript">
document.write("Hello World!");
</script>
</body>
</html>
```

Program 15.2
Usage of <script> tag

```
<html>
<head>
```

```
<title>Usage of script tag.</title>
</head>
<body>
<script type="text/javascript">
window.alert("Hello World!");
</script>
</body>
</html>
```

Program 15.3

Usage of <script> tag

```
<html>
<head>
<title>Usage of script tag.</title>
</head>
<body>
<script type="text/vbscript">
MsgBox "Hello World!"
</script>
</body>
</html>
```

Program 15.4

Usage of <script> tag

```
<html>
<head>
<title>Usage of script tag.</title>
<script type="text/javascript">
function funClick()
{
window.alert("Hello World!")
}
</script>
</head>
<body>
<input type="button" value="click" onClick="funClick()">
```

```
</body>
</html>
```

Program 15.5

Usage of <script> tag

```
<html>
<head>
<title>Usage of script tag.</title>
<script type="text/vbscript">
funClick()
{
MsgBox "Hello World!"
}
</script>
</head>
<body>
<input type="button" value="click" onClick="funClick()">
</body>
</html>
```

Program 15.6

Usage of <script> tag

```
<html>
<head>
<title>Usage of <noscript> tag.</title>
</head>
<body>
<script>
document.write("Hello World!")
</script>
<noscript>Your browser does not support JavaScript!</noscript>
</body>
</html>
```

PART - II

CSS

Programming

HTML & CSS

Programming Guide

Chapter 16

Cascading Style Sheets

16. Cascading Style Sheets

Cascading Style Sheets, fondly referred to as CSS, is a simple design language intended to simplify the process of making web pages presentable. CSS handles the look and feel part of a web page. Using CSS, we can control the color of the text, the style of fonts, the spacing between paragraphs, how columns are sized and laid out, what background images or colors are used, as well as a variety of other effects. CSS is easy to learn and understand but it provides powerful control over the presentation of an HTML document. Most commonly, CSS is combined with the markup languages HTML or XHTML.

A CSS comprises of style rules that are interpreted by the browser and then applied to the corresponding elements in your document. A style rule is made of three parts:

- **Selector:** A selector is an HTML tag at which style will be applied. This could be any tag like <h1> or <table> etc.
- **Property:** A property is a type of attribute of HTML tag. Put simply, all the HTML attributes are converted into CSS properties. They could be color or border etc.
- **Value:** Values are assigned to properties. For example color property can have value either red or #F1F1F1 etc.

Syntax:

selector { property: value }

Example:

table { border :1px solid #C00; }

Here table is a selector and border is a property and given value 1px solid #C00 is the value of that property. We can define selectors in various simple ways based on comfort.

The Type Selectors:

This is the same selector we have seen above. Again one more example to give a color to all level 1 headings :

```
h1 {
    color: #36CFFF;
}
```

The Universal Selectors:

Rather than selecting elements of a specific type, the universal selector quite simply matches the name of any element type :

```
* {
    color: #000000;
}
```

This rule renders the content of every element in our document in black.

The Descendant Selectors:

Suppose we want to apply a style rule to a particular element only when it lies inside a particular element. As given in the following example, style rule will apply to <em> element only when it lies inside <ul> tag.

```
ul em {
    color: #000000;
}
```

The Class Selectors:

We can define style rules based on the class attribute of the elements. All the elements having that class will be formatted according to the defined rule.

```
.black {
    color: #000000;
}
```

This rule renders the content in black for every element with class attribute set to black in our document. We can make it a bit more particular. For example:

```
h1.black {
    color: #000000;
}
```

This rule renders the content in black for only <h1> elements with class attribute set to black. We can apply more than one class selectors to given element. Consider the following example:

```
<p class="center bold">
This para will be styled by the classes center and bold.
</p>
```

The ID Selectors:
We can define style rules based on the id attribute of the elements. All the elements having that id will be formatted according to the defined rule.

```
#black {
  color: #000000;
}
```

This rule renders the content in black for every element with id attribute set to black in our document. We can make it a bit more particular. For example:

```
h1#black {
  color: #000000;
}
```

This rule renders the content in black for only <h1> elements with id attribute set to black.

The true power of id selectors is when they are used as the foundation for descendant selectors, For example:

```
#black h2 {
  color: #000000;
}
```

In this example all level 2 headings will be displayed in black color only when those headings will lie with in tags having id attribute set to black.

The Child Selectors:

We have seen descendant selectors. There is one more type of selectors which is very similar to descendants but have different functionality. Consider the following example:

```
body > p {
  color: #000000;
}
```

This rule will render all the paragraphs in black if they are direct child of <body> element. Other paragraphs put inside other elements like <div> or <td> etc. would not have any effect of this rule.

The Attribute Selectors:

We can also apply styles to HTML elements with particular attributes. The style rule below will match all input elements that has a type attribute with a value of text:

```
input[type="text"]{
  color: #000000;
}
```

The advantage to this method is that the <input type="submit" /> element is unaffected, and the color applied only to the desired text fields.

Multiple Style Rules:

We may need to define multiple style rules for a single element. We can define these rules to combine multiple properties and corresponding values into a single block as defined in the following example:

```
h1 {
color: #36C;
font-weight: normal;
letter-spacing: .4em;
margin-bottom: 1em;
text-transform: lowercase;
}
```

Here all the property and value pairs are separated by a semi colon (;). You can keep them in a single line or multiple lines. For better readability we keep them into separate lines.

Grouping Selectors:

We can apply a style to many selectors as we like. Just separate the selectors with a comma as given in the following example:

```
h1, h2, h3 {
color: #36C;
font-weight: normal;
letter-spacing: .4em;
margin-bottom: 1em;
text-transform: lowercase;
}
```

This define style rule will be applicable to h1, h2 and h3 element as well. The order of the list is irrelevant. All the elements in the selector will have the corresponding declarations applied to them.

We can combine various class selectors together as shown below:

```
#content, #footer, #supplement {
position: absolute;
left: 510px;
width: 200px;
}
```

CSS Units & Measurements

CSS supports a number of measurements including absolute units such as inches, centimeters, points, and so on, as well as relative measures such as percentages and em units. We need these values while specifying various measurements in the Style rules e.g border="1px solid red".

We have listed out all the CSS Measurement Units along with proper examples:

Unit	Description	Example
%	Defines a measurement as a percentage relative to another value, typically an enclosing element.	p {font-size: 16pt; line-height: 125%;}
cm	Defines a measurement in centimeters.	div {margin-bottom: 2cm;}
em	A relative measurement for the height of a font in em spaces. Because an em unit is equivalent to the size of a given font, if you assign a font to 12pt, each "em" unit would be 12pt; thus, 2em would be 24pt.	p {letter-spacing: 7em;}
ex	This value defines a measurement relative to a font's x-height. The x-height is determined by the height of the font's lowercase letter x.	p {font-size: 24pt; line-height: 3ex;}
in	Defines a measurement in inches.	p {word-spacing: .15in;}
mm	Defines a measurement in millimeters.	p {word-spacing: 15mm;}
pc	Defines a measurement in picas. A pica is equivalent to 12 points; thus, there are 6 picas per inch.	p {font-size: 20pc;}
pt	Defines a measurement in points. A point is defined as 1/72nd of an inch.	body {font-size: 18pt;}
px	Defines a measurement in screen pixels.	p {padding: 25px;}

HTML & CSS

Programming Guide

Chapter 17

Font Styles

17. Font Styles

font	It defines all the font properties in one declaration. *Values:* • font-family • font-size • font-style • font-variant • font-weight • font-stretch
font-family	It defines the font family of the text. *Values:* • family-name • generic-family • inherit
font-size	It defines the font size of the text. *Values:* • xx-small • x-small • small • medium • large • x-large • xx-large • smaller • larger • inherit • length • %
font-style	It defines the font style of the text. *Values:* • normal • italic • oblique

	• inherit
font-variant	It defines the font variant of the text. *Values:* • normal • small-caps • inherit
font-weight	It defines the font weight of the text. *Values:* • normal • bold • bolder • lighter • Inherit
font-stretch	It defines the font stretch ratio of the text. *Values:* • normal • wider • narrower • ultra-condensed • extra-condensed • condensed • semi-condensed • semi-expanded • expanded • extra-expanded • ultra-expanded • inherit

Coding Snippets:

Program 17.1

Usage of font-family property

```
<html>
<head>
<title>Usage of font-family Property</title>
```

```
<style>
p.one{font-family:Times New Roman,Times,serif;}
p.two{font-family:Arial,Helvetica,sans-serif;}
</style>
</head>
<body>
<h1>font-family property</h1>
<p class="one">Sample Text - Times New Roman font.</p>
<p class="two">Sample Text - Arial font.</p>
</body>
</html>
```

Program 17.2

Usage of font-size property

```
<html>
<head>
<title>Usage of font-size Property</title>
<style>
h1 {font-size:250%;}
h2 {font-size:200%;}
p {font-size:100%;}
</style>
</head>
<body>
<h1>Heading 1 Text</h1>
<h2>Heading 2 Text</h2>
<p>Paragraph Text</p>
</body>
</html>
```

Program 17.3

Usage of font-size property

```
<html>
<head>
<title>Usage of font-size Property</title>
<style>
```

```
h1 {font-size:50px;}
h2 {font-size:40px;}
p {font-size:20px;}
</style>
</head>
<body>
<h1>Heading 1 Text</h1>
<h2>Heading 2 Text</h2>
<p>Paragraph Text</p>
</body>
</html>
```

Program 17.4

Usage of font-size property

```
<html>
<head>
<title>Usage of font-size Property</title>
<style>
h1 {font-size:3.12em;}
h2 {font-size:2.5em;}
p {font-size:1.25em;}
</style>
</head>
<body>
<h1>Heading 1 Text</h1>
<h2>Heading 2 Text</h2>
<p>Paragraph Text</p>
</body>
</html>
```

Program 17.5

Usage of font-size property

```
<html>
<head>
<title>Usage of font-size Property</title>
<style>
```

```
h1 {font-size:xx-large;}
h2 {font-size:x-large;}
h3 {font-size:large;}
h4 {font-size:medium;}
h5 {font-size:small;}
h6 {font-size:x-small;}
p {font-size:xx-small;}
</style>
</head>
<body>
<h1>Heading 1 Text : xx-large</h1>
<h2>Heading 2 Text : x-large</h2>
<h3>Heading 3 Text : large</h3>
<h4>Heading 4 Text : medium</h4>
<h5>Heading 5 Text : small</h5>
<h6>Heading 6 Text : x-small</h6>
<p>Paragraph Text : xx-small</p>
</body>
</html>
```

Program 17.6

Usage of font-style property

```
<html>
<head>
<title>Usage of font-style Property</title>
<style>
p.normal {font-style:normal;}
p.italic {font-style:italic;}
p.oblique {font-style:oblique;}
</style>
</head>
<body>
<p class="normal">Sample Text - normal.</p>
<p class="italic">Sample Text - italic.</p>
<p class="oblique">Sample Text - oblique.</p>
</body>
</html>
```

Program 17.7

Usage of font-variant property

```
<html>
<head>
<title>Usage of font-variant Property</title>
<style>
p.normal {font-variant:normal;}
p.smallcaps {font-variant:small-caps;}
</style>
</head>
<body>
<p class="normal">Paragraph Text - normal</p>
<p class="smallcaps">Paragraph Text - smallcaps</p>
</body>
</html>
```

Program 17.8

Usage of font properties in one declaration

```
<html>
<head>
<title>Usage of font Properties</title>
<style>
p.one {font:15px arial,sans-serif;}
p.two {font:italic bold 15px Georgia,serif;}
</style>
</head>
<body>
<p class="one">Paragraph Text</p>
<p class="two">Paragraph Text</p>
</body>
</html>
```

HTML & CSS

Programming Guide

Chapter 18

Text Styles

18. Text Styles

color	It defines the color of the text. *Values:* • color • inherit
direction	It defines the direction of the text. *Values:* • ltr • rtl • inherit
letter-spacing	It defines the space between the characters of the text. *Values:* • normal • length • inherit
line-height	It defines the line height between two lines. *Values:* • normal • length • % • inherit
text-align	It defines the horizontal alignment of the text. *Values:* • left • right • center • justify • inherit
text-decoration	It defines the decoration added to the text. *Values:* • none

	• underline • overline • line-through • blink • inherit
text-emphasis	It defines emphasis marks, and the foreground color of the emphasis marks to the text. *Values:* • none • accent [before/after] • dot [before/after] • circle [before/after] • disc [before/after]
text-indent	It defines the indentation of the text block. *Values:* • length • %
text-justify	It defines the justification method of text. *Values:* • auto • inter-word • inter-ideograph • inter-cluster • distribute • kashida • Tibetan • none
text-outline	It defines the text outline. *Values:* • none • color • length
text-overflow	It defines what should happen when text overflows the containing element.

	Values:
	• clip
	• ellipsis
	• string
text-shadow	It adds shadow effect to the text.
	Values:
	• none
	• color
	• length
text-transform	It defines the capitalization effect of the text.
	Values:
	• none
	• capitalize
	• uppercase
	• lowercase
text-wrap	It defines the breaking rules of the text.
	Values:
	• normal
	• unrestricted
	• none
	• suppress
vertical-align	It defines the vertical alignment of an element.
	Values:
	• length
	• %
	• baseline
	• sub
	• super
	• top
	• text-top
	• middle
	• bottom
	• text-bottom
	• inherit

white-space	It defines how the whitespace inside a text handled. *Values:* <ul><li>normal</li><li>nowrap</li><li>pre</li><li>pre-line</li><li>pre-wrap</li><li>inherit</li></ul>
word-break	It defines the breaking rules of a line. *Values:* <ul><li>normal</li><li>keep-all</li><li>loose</li><li>break-strict</li><li>break-all</li></ul>
word-spacing	It defines the space between the words in a line. *Values:* <ul><li>normal</li><li>length</li><li>inherit</li></ul>
word-wrap	It helps to wrap the non-breakable words to the next line. *Values:* <ul><li>normal</li><li>break-word</li></ul>

Coding Snippets:

Program 18.1

Usage of the color property

```
<html>
<head>
<title>Usage of color property</title>
<style>
body {color:red;}
```

```
h1 {color:#00ff00;}
p.one {color:rgb(0,0,255);}
</style>
</head>
<body>
<h1>Heading Text 1 - Green Color</h1>
<p>Paragraph Text 1 - Red Color</p>
<p class="one">Paragraph Text 1 - Blue Color</p>
</body>
</html>
```

Program 18.2

Usage of the direction property

```
<html>
<head>
<title>Usage of direction property</title>
<style>
p.normal {direction:none;}
p.rtl {direction:rtl;}
p.ltr {direction:ltr;}
</style>
</head>
<body>
<p class="none">Text with default direction.</p>
<p class="rtl">Text with right-to-left direction.</p>
<p class="ltr">Text with left-to-right direction.</p>
</body>
</html>
```

Program 18.3

Usage of the letter-spacing property

```
<html>
<head>
<title>Usage of letter-spacing property</title>
<style>
p.one {letter-spacing:2px;}
```

```
p.two {letter-spacing:-3px;}
</style>
</head>
<body>
<p>Paragraph text with normal letter spacing.</p>
<p class="one">Paragraph text with letter spacing 2px.</p>
<p class="two">Paragraph text with letter spacing -3px.</p>
</body>
</html>
```

Program 18.4

Usage of the line-height property

```
<html>
<head>
<title>Usage of line-height property</title>
<style>
p.small {line-height:60%;}
p.big {line-height:250%;}
</style>
</head>
<body>
<p>
Paragraph text with standard line-height.<br>
Paragraph text with standard line-height.<br>
Paragraph text with standard line-height.<br>
</p>
<p class="small">
Paragraph text with smaller line-height - 60%.<br>
Paragraph text with smaller line-height - 60%.<br>
Paragraph text with smaller line-height - 60%.<br>
Paragraph text with smaller line-height - 60%.<br>
</p>
<p class="big">
Paragraph text with bigger line-height - 250%.<br>
Paragraph text with bigger line-height - 250%.<br>
Paragraph text with bigger line-height - 250%.<br>
Paragraph text with bigger line-height - 250%.<br>
```

```
</p>
</body>
</html>
```

Program 18.5

Usage of the line-height property

```
<html>
<head>
<title>Usage of line-height property</title>
<style>
p.small {line-height:10px;}
p.big {line-height:30px;}
</style>
</head>
<body>
<p>
Paragraph text with standard line-height.<br>
Paragraph text with standard line-height.<br>
Paragraph text with standard line-height.<br>
</p>
<p class="small">
Paragraph text with smaller line-height - 10px.<br>
Paragraph text with smaller line-height - 10px.<br>
Paragraph text with smaller line-height - 10px.<br>
Paragraph text with smaller line-height - 10px.<br>
</p>
<p class="big">
Paragraph text with bigger line-height - 30px.<br>
Paragraph text with bigger line-height - 30px.<br>
Paragraph text with bigger line-height - 30px.<br>
Paragraph text with bigger line-height - 30px.<br>
</p>
</body>
</html>
```

Program 18.6

Usage of the text-align property

```
<html>
<head>
<title>Usage of text-align property</title>
<style>
h1 {text-align:center;}
p.date {text-align:right;}
p.name {text-align:left;}
p.main {text-align:justify;}
</style>
</head>
<body>
<h1>HTML - Hyper Text Markup Language</h1>
<p class="date">14 June, 2013</p>
<p class="main">
HTML - Hyper Text Markup Language is the predominant markup
language for designing web pages.  It provides a means to describe the
structure of text-based information in a document - by denoting certain
text as links, headings, paragraphs, lists, and so on - and to supplement
that text with interactive forms, embedded images, and other objects.
</p>
<p class="name">- Venkatesh Ramasamy</p>
</body>
</html>
```

Program 18.7

Usage of the text-decoration property

```
<html>
<head>
<title>Usage of text-decoration property</title>
<style>
p.overline {text-decoration:overline;}
p.linethrough {text-decoration:line-through;}
p.underline {text-decoration:underline;}
p.blink {text-decoration:blink;}
```

```
</style>
</head>
<body>
<p class="overline">Paragraph text with overline text decoration</p>
<p class="linethrough">Paragraph text with line-through text decoration</p>
<p class="underline">Paragraph text with underline text decoration</p>
<p class="blink">Paragraph text with blink text decoration</p>
</body>
</html>
```

Program 18.8

Usage of the text-decoration property

```
<html>
<head>
<title>Usage of text-decoration property</title>
<style>
a {text-decoration:none;}
</style>
</head>
<body>
<p><a href="http://www.google.com">Google Site</a></p>
</body>
</html>
```

Program 18.9

Usage of the text-indent property

```
<html>
<head>
<title>Usage of text-indent property</title>
<style>
p {text-indent:50px;}
</style>
</head>
<body>
<p>
```

HTML - Hyper Text Markup Language is the predominant markup language for designing web pages. It provides a means to describe the structure of text-based information in a document - by denoting certain text as links, headings, paragraphs, lists, and so on - and to supplement that text with interactive forms, embedded images, and other objects.
</p>
</body>
</html>

Program 18.10

Usage of the text-indent property

```
<html>
<head>
<title>Usage of text-indent property</title>
<style>
p {text-indent:15%;}
</style>
</head>
<body>
<p>
```
HTML - Hyper Text Markup Language is the predominant markup language for designing web pages. It provides a means to describe the structure of text-based information in a document - by denoting certain text as links, headings, paragraphs, lists, and so on - and to supplement that text with interactive forms, embedded images, and other objects.
</p>
</body>
</html>

Program 18.11

Usage of the text-justify property

```
<html>
<head>
<title>Usage of text-justify property</title>
<style>
p.interword
```

```
{
text-align:justify;
text-justify:inter-word;
}
p.interideograph
{
text-align:justify;
text-justify:inter-ideograph;
}
p.intercluster
{
text-align:justify;
text-justify:inter-cluster;
}
p.distribute
{
text-align:justify;
text-justify:distribute;
}
p.kashida
{
text-align:justify;
text-justify:kashida;
}
p.tibetan
{
text-align:justify;
text-justify:tibetan;
}
p.none
{
text-align:justify;
text-justify:none;
}
</style>
</head>
<body>
<p class="interword">
```

HTML provides a means to describe the structure of text-based information in a document - by denoting certain text as links, headings, paragraphs, lists, and so on - and to supplement that text with interactive forms, embedded images, and other objects.
</p>
<p class="interideograph">
HTML provides a means to describe the structure of text-based information in a document - by denoting certain text as links, headings, paragraphs, lists, and so on - and to supplement that text with interactive forms, embedded images, and other objects.
</p>
<p class="intercluster">
HTML provides a means to describe the structure of text-based information in a document - by denoting certain text as links, headings, paragraphs, lists, and so on - and to supplement that text with interactive forms, embedded images, and other objects.
</p>
<p class="distribute">
HTML provides a means to describe the structure of text-based information in a document - by denoting certain text as links, headings, paragraphs, lists, and so on - and to supplement that text with interactive forms, embedded images, and other objects.
</p>
<p class="kashida">
HTML provides a means to describe the structure of text-based information in a document - by denoting certain text as links, headings, paragraphs, lists, and so on - and to supplement that text with interactive forms, embedded images, and other objects.
</p>
<p class="tibetan">
HTML provides a means to describe the structure of text-based information in a document - by denoting certain text as links, headings, paragraphs, lists, and so on - and to supplement that text with interactive forms, embedded images, and other objects.
</p>
<p class="none">
HTML provides a means to describe the structure of text-based information in a document - by denoting certain text as links, headings,

paragraphs, lists, and so on - and to supplement that text with interactive forms, embedded images, and other objects.

```
</p>
</body>
</html>
```

Program 18.12

Usage of the text-overflow property

```
<html>
<head>
<title>Usage of text-overflow property</title>
<style>
p.ex1
{
white-space:nowrap;
width:12em;
overflow:hidden;
border:1px solid #000000;
text-overflow:ellipsis;
}
p.ex2
{
white-space:nowrap;
width:12em;
overflow:hidden;
border:1px solid #000000;
text-overflow:clip;
}
</style>
</head>
<body>
<p class="ex1">This is some long text that will not fit in the box.</p>
<p class="ex2">This is some long text that will not fit in the box.</p>
</body>
</html>
```

Program 18.13

Usage of the text-shadow property

```
<html>
<head>
<title>Usage of text-shadow property</title>
<style>
h1 {text-shadow:2px 2px #FF0000;}
</style>
</head>
<body>
<h1>text-shadow effect</h1>
</body>
</html>
```

Program 18.14

Usage of the text-shadow property

```
<html>
<head>
<title>Usage of text-shadow property</title>
<style>
h1 {text-shadow:4px 4px #00FF00;}
</style>
</head>
<body>
<h1>text-shadow effect</h1>
</body>
</html>
```

Program 18.15

Usage of the text-transform property

```
<html>
<head>
<title>Usage of text-transform property</title>
<style>
p.uppercase {text-transform:uppercase;}
```

```
p.lowercase {text-transform:lowercase;}
p.capitalize {text-transform:capitalize;}
</style>
</head>
<body>
<p class="uppercase">Paragraph Text - Uppercase</p>
<p class="lowercase">Paragraph Text - Lowercase</p>
<p class="capitalize">Paragraph Text - Capitalize</p>
</body>
</html>
```

Program 18.16

Usage of the vertical-align property

```
<html>
<head>
<title>Usage of vertical-align property</title>
<style>
span.length {vertical-align:10px;}
span.percent {vertical-align:30%;}
span.baseline {vertical-align:baseline;}
span.sub {vertical-align:sub;}
span.super {vertical-align:super;}
span.top {vertical-align:top;}
span.texttop {vertical-align:text-top;}
span.middle {vertical-align:middle;}
span.bottom {vertical-align:bottom;}
span.textbottom {vertical-align:text-bottom;}
</style>
</head>
<body>
<table border="1">
<tr style="height:60px;">
<td>Hi <span class="length">Sample Text : 10px in length </span></td>
</tr>
<tr style="height:60px;">
<td>Hi <span class="percent">Sample Text : 30% in
percent</span></td>
```

```
</tr>
<tr style="height:60px;">
<td>Hi <span class="baseline">Sample Text : baseline</span></td>
</tr>
<tr style="height:60px;">
<td>Hi <span class="sub">Sample Text : sub</span></td>
</tr>
<tr style="height:60px;">
<td>Hi <span class="super">Sample Text : super</span></td>
</tr>
<tr style="height:60px;">
<td>Hi <span class="top">Sample Text : top</span></td>
</tr>
<tr style="height:60px;">
<td>Hi <span class="text-top">Sample Text : text-top</span></td>
</tr>
<tr style="height:60px;">
<td>Hi <span class="middle">Sample Text : middle</span></td>
</tr>
<tr style="height:60px;">
<td>Hi <span class="bottom">Sample Text : bottom</span></td>
</tr>
<tr style="height:60px;">
<td>Hi <span class="text-bottom">Sample Text : text-
bottom</span></td>
</tr>
</table>
</body>
</html>
```

Program 18.17
Usage of the white-space property

```
<html>
<head>
<title>Usage of white-space property</title>
<style>
p.ex1
```

```
{
white-space:normal;
}
p.ex2
{
white-space:nowrap;
}
p.ex3
{
white-space:pre;
}
p.ex4
{
white-space:pre-line;
}
p.ex5
{
white-space:pre-wrap;
}
</style>
</head>
<body>
<p class="ex1">
Paragraph Text 1. Paragraph Text 1. Paragraph Text 1.
Paragraph Text 1. Paragraph Text 1. Paragraph Text 1.
Paragraph Text 1. Paragraph Text 1. Paragraph Text 1.
</p>
<p class="ex2">
Paragraph Text 2. Paragraph Text 2. Paragraph Text 2.
Paragraph Text 2. Paragraph Text 2. Paragraph Text 2.
Paragraph Text 2. Paragraph Text 2. Paragraph Text 2.
</p>
<p class="ex3">
Paragraph Text 3. Paragraph Text 3. Paragraph Text 3.
Paragraph Text 3. Paragraph Text 3. Paragraph Text 3.
Paragraph Text 3. Paragraph Text 3. Paragraph Text 3.
</p>
```

```
<p class="ex4">
Paragraph Text 4. Paragraph Text 4. Paragraph Text 4.
Paragraph Text 4. Paragraph Text 4. Paragraph Text 4.
Paragraph Text 4. Paragraph Text 4. Paragraph Text 4.
</p>
<p class="ex5">
Paragraph Text 5. Paragraph Text 5. Paragraph Text 5.
Paragraph Text 5. Paragraph Text 5. Paragraph Text 5.
Paragraph Text 5. Paragraph Text 5. Paragraph Text 5.
</p>
</body>
</html>
```

Program 18.18

Usage of the word-spacing property

```
<html>
<head>
<title>Usage of word-spacing property</title>
<style>
p.ex1
{
word-spacing:10px;
}
p.ex2
{
word-spacing:30px;
}
</style>
</head>
<body>
<p class="ex1">
This is sample text. This is sample text.
</p>
<p class="ex2">
This is sample text. This is sample text.
</p>
</body></html>
```

Program 18.19

Usage of the word-break property

```
<html>
<head>
<title>Usage of word-break property</title>
<style>
p.ex1
{
width:250px;
border:1px solid #000000;
word-break:hyphenate;
}
p.ex2
{
width:250px;
border:1px solid #000000;
word-break:break-all;
}
</style>
</head>
<body>
<p class="ex1">
HTML provides a means to describe the structure of text-based
information in a document - by denoting certain text as links, headings,
paragraphs, lists, and so on - and to supplement that text with
interactive forms, embedded images, and other objects.
</p>
<p class="ex2">
HTML provides a means to describe the structure of text-based
information in a document - by denoting certain text as links, headings,
paragraphs, lists, and so on - and to supplement that text with
interactive forms, embedded images, and other objects.
</p>
</body>
</html>
```

Program 18.20

Usage of the word-wrap property

```
<html>
<head>
<style>
p.ex1
{
width:150px;
border:1px solid #000000;
word-wrap:none;
}
p.ex2
{
width:150px;
border:1px solid #000000;
word-wrap:break-word;
}
</style>
</head>
<body>
<p class="ex1">
HTML provides a means to describe the structure of text-based
information in a document - bydenotingcertaintextaslinks,headings,
paragraphs, lists, and so on - and to supplement that text with
interactive forms, embedded images, and other objects.
</p>
<p class="ex2">
HTML provides a means to describe the structure of text-based
information in a document - bydenotingcertaintextaslinks,headings,
paragraphs, lists, and so on - and to supplement that text with
interactive forms, embedded images, and other objects.
</p>
</body>
</html>
```

HTML & CSS

Programming Guide

Chapter 19

List Styles

19. List Styles

list-style	It defines all the properties for a list in one declaration. *Values:* • list-style-type • list-style-position • list-style-image
list-style-image	It defines an image as list item placeholder. *Values:* • url • none • inherit
list-style-position	It defines whether the list item placeholder should appear inside or outside the content flow. *Values:* • inside • outside • inherit
list-style-type	It defines the style of list item type. *Values:* • none • asterisks • box • check • circle • diamond • disc • hyphen • square • decimal • decimal-leading-zero • lower-roman • upper-roman

- lower-alpha
- upper-alpha
- lower-greek
- lower-latin
- upper-latin
- hebrew
- armenian
- georgian
- cjk-ideographic
- hiragana
- katakana
- hira-gana-iroha
- katakana-iroha
- footnotes

Coding Snippets:

Program 19.1

Usage of list-style-type property in Un-ordered List

```
<html>
<head>
<title>Usage of list-style-type property in Un-ordered List</title>
<style>
ul.a {list-style-type:asterisks;}
ul.b {list-style-type:box;}
ul.c {list-style-type:check;}
ul.d {list-style-type:circle;}
ul.e {list-style-type:diamond;}
ul.f {list-style-type:hypen;}
ul.g {list-style-type:square;}
</style>
</head>
<body>
<ul class="a">
<li>Asterisks Type Text 01</li>
<li>Asterisks Type Text 02</li>
```

```
<li>Asterisks Type Text 03</li>
</ul>
<ul class="b">
<li>Box Type Text 01</li>
<li>Box Type Text 02</li>
<li>Box Type Text 03</li>
</ul>
<ul class="c">
<li>Check Type Text 01</li>
<li>Check Type Text 02</li>
<li>Check Type Text 03</li>
</ul>
<ul class="d">
<li>Circle Type Text 01</li>
<li>Circle Type Text 02</li>
<li>Circle Type Text 03</li>
</ul>
<ul class="e">
<li>Diamond Type Text 01</li>
<li>Diamond Type Text 02</li>
<li>Diamond Type Text 03</li>
</ul>
<ul class="f">
<li>Hypen Type Text 01</li>
<li>Hypen Type Text 02</li>
<li>Hypen Type Text 03</li>
</ul>
<ul class="g">
<li>Square Type Text 01</li>
<li>Square Type Text 02</li>
<li>Square Type Text 03</li>
</ul>
</body>
</html>
```

Program 19.2

Usage of list-style-type property in Ordered List

```
<html>
<head>
<title>Usage of list-style-type Property in Ordered List</title>
<style>
ol.a {list-style-type:decimal;}
ol.b {list-style-type:decimal-leading-zero;}
ol.c {list-style-type:lower-roman;}
ol.d {list-style-type:upper-roman;}
ol.e {list-style-type:lower-alpha;}
ol.f {list-style-type:upper-alpha;}
ol.g {list-style-type:lower-greek;}
ol.h {list-style-type:upper-greek;}
ol.i {list-style-type:lower-latin;}
ol.j {list-style-type:upper-latin;}
ol.k {list-style-type:hebrew;}
ol.l {list-style-type:armenian;}
ol.m {list-style-type:georgian;}
ol.n {list-style-type:cjk-ideographic;}
ol.o {list-style-type:hiragana;}
ol.p {list-style-type:katakana;}
ol.q {list-style-type:hira-gana-iroha;}
ol.r {list-style-type:katakana-iroha;}
ol.s {list-style-type:footnotes;}
</style>
</head>
<body>
<ol class="a">
<li>Decimal Type Text 01</li>
<li>Decimal Type Text 02</li>
<li>Decimal Type Text 03</li>
</ol>
<ol class="b">
<li>decimal-leading-zero Type Text 01</li>
<li>decimal-leading-zero Type Text 02</li>
<li>decimal-leading-zero Type Text 03</li>
```

```
</ol>
<ol class="c">
<li>lower-roman Type Text 01</li>
<li>lower-roman Type Text 02</li>
<li>lower-roman Type Text 03</li>
</ol>
<ol class="d">
<li>upper-roman Type Text 01</li>
<li>upper-roman Type Text 02</li>
<li>upper-roman Type Text 03</li>
</ol>
<ol class="e">
<li>lower-alpha Type Text 01</li>
<li>lower-alpha Type Text 02</li>
<li>lower-alpha Type Text 03</li>
</ol>
<ol class="f">
<li>upper-alpha Type Text 01</li>
<li>upper-alpha Type Text 02</li>
<li>upper-alpha Type Text 03</li>
</ol>
<ol class="g">
<li>lower-greek Type Text 01</li>
<li>lower-greek Type Text 02</li>
<li>lower-greek Type Text 03</li>
</ol>
<ol class="h">
<li>upper-greek Type Text 01</li>
<li>upper-greek Type Text 02</li>
<li>upper-greek Type Text 03</li>
</ol>
<ol class="i">
<li>lower-latin Type Text 01</li>
<li>lower-latin Type Text 02</li>
<li>lower-latin Type Text 03</li>
</ol>
<ol class="j">
<li>upper-latin Type Text 01</li>
```

```
<li>upper-latin Type Text 02</li>
<li>upper-latin Type Text 03</li>
</ol>
<ol class="k">
<li>hebrew Type Text 01</li>
<li>hebrew Type Text 02</li>
<li>hebrew Type Text 03</li>
</ol>
<ol class="l">
<li>armenian Type Text 01</li>
<li>armenian Type Text 02</li>
<li>armenian Type Text 03</li>
</ol>
<ol class="m">
<li>georgian Type Text 01</li>
<li>georgian Type Text 02</li>
<li>georgian Type Text 03</li>
</ol>
<ol class="n">
<li>cjk-ideographic Type Text 01</li>
<li>cjk-ideographic Type Text 02</li>
<li>cjk-ideographic Type Text 03</li>
</ol>
<ol class="o">
<li>hiragana Type Text 01</li>
<li>hiragana Type Text 02</li>
<li>hiragana Type Text 03</li>
</ol>
<ol class="p">
<li>katakana Type Text 01</li>
<li>katakana Type Text 02</li>
<li>katakana Type Text 03</li>
</ol>
<ol class="q">
<li>hira-gana-iroha Type Text 01</li>
<li>hira-gana-iroha Type Text 02</li>
<li>hira-gana-iroha Type Text 03</li>
</ol>
```

```
<ol class="r">
<li>katakana-iroha Type Text 01</li>
<li>katakana-iroha Type Text 02</li>
<li>katakana-iroha Type Text 03</li>
</ol>
<ol class="s">
<li>footnotes Type Text 01</li>
<li>footnotes Type Text 02</li>
<li>footnotes Type Text 03</li>
</ol>
</body>
</html>
```

Program 19.3

Usage of list-style-image property in Ordered List

```
<html>
<head>
<title>Usage of list-style-image Property</title>
<style>
ul
{
list-style-image:url('squarelistitem.gif');
}
</style>
</head>
<body>
<ul>
<li>Sample Text 01</li>
<li>Sample Text 02</li>
<li>Sample Text 03</li>
</ul>
</body>
</html>
```

Program 19.4

Usage of list-style-position property in Ordered List

```
<html>
<head>
<title>Usage of list-style-position Property</title>
<style>
ul.a
{
list-style-image:url('squarelistitem.gif')
list-style-position: inside;
}
ul.b
{
list-style-image:url('squarelistitem.gif')
list-style-position: outside;
}
</style>
</head>
<body>
<ul class="a">
<li>Sample Text 01</li>
<li>Sample Text 02</li>
<li>Sample Text 03</li>
</ul>
<ul class="b">
<li>Sample Text 01</li>
<li>Sample Text 02</li>
<li>Sample Text 03</li>
</ul>
</body>
</html>
```

Program 19.5

Usage of list-style property in Ordered List

```
<html>
<head>
```

```
<title>Usage of list-style Property</title>
<style>
ul
{
list-style:square url("sqpurple.gif");
}
</style>
</head>
<body>
<ul>
<li>Sample Text 01</li>
<li>Sample Text 02</li>
<li>Sample Text 03</li>
</ul>
</body>
</html>
```

HTML & CSS

Programming Guide

Chapter 20

Link Styles

20. Link Styles

a:link	It defines a normal, unvisited link.
a:visited	It defines a link the user has visited.
a:hover	It defines a link when the user mouse's over it.
a:active	It defines a link the moment it is clicked.

Coding Snippets:

Program 20.1

Usage of link style properties

```
<!DOCTYPE html>
<html>
<head>
<style>
a:link {color:#FF0000;}    /* unvisited link */
a:visited {color:#00FF00;} /* visited link */
a:hover {color:#FF00FF;}   /* mouse over link */
a:active {color:#0000FF;}  /* selected link */
</style>
</head>
<body>
<p><b><a href="http://www.google.com" target="_blank"> Google Link
</a></b></p>
</body>
</html>
```

Program 20.2

Usage of link style properties

```
<!DOCTYPE html>
<html>
<head>
<style>
```

```
a:link {text-decoration:none;}    /* unvisited link */
a:visited {text-decoration:none;} /* visited link */
a:hover {text-decoration:underline;}   /* mouse over link */
a:active {text-decoration:underline;}  /* selected link */
</style>
</head>
<body>
<p><b><a href="http://www.google.com" target="_blank"> Google Link
</a></b></p>
</body>
</html>
```

Program 20.3

Usage of link style properties

```
<!DOCTYPE html>
<html>
<head>
<style>
a:link {background-color:#B2FF99;}    /* unvisited link */
a:visited {background-color:#FFFF85;} /* visited link */
a:hover {background-color:#FF704D;}   /* mouse over link */
a:active {background-color:#FF704D;}  /* selected link */
</style>
</head>
<body>
<p><b><a href="http://www.google.com" target="_blank"> Google Link
</a></b></p>
</body>
</html>
```

Program 20.4

Usage of link style properties

```
<!DOCTYPE html>
<html>
<head>
<style>
```

```
a.one:link {color:#ff0000;}
a.one:visited {color:#0000ff;}
a.one:hover {color:#ffcc00;}

a.two:link {color:#ff0000;}
a.two:visited {color:#0000ff;}
a.two:hover {font-size:150%;}

a.three:link {color:#ff0000;}
a.three:visited {color:#0000ff;}
a.three:hover {background:#66ff66;}

a.four:link {color:#ff0000;}
a.four:visited {color:#0000ff;}
a.four:hover {font-family:monospace;}

a.five:link {color:#ff0000;text-decoration:none;}
a.five:visited {color:#0000ff;text-decoration:none;}
a.five:hover {text-decoration:underline;}

</style>
</head>
<body>
<p>Mouse over the links to see them change layout.</p>
<p><b><a class="one" href=" http://www.google.com" target="_blank">
Google Link</a></b></p>
<p><b><a class="two" href=" http://www.google.com" target="_blank">
Google Link</a></b></p>
<p><b><a class="three" href=" http://www.google.com" target="_blank">
Google Link</a></b></p>
<p><b><a class="four" href=" http://www.google.com" target="_blank">
Google Link</a></b></p>
<p><b><a class="five" href=" http://www.google.com" target="_blank">
Google Link</a></b></p>
</body>
</html>
```

Program 20.5

Usage of link style properties

```
<!DOCTYPE html>
<html>
<head>
<style>
a:link,a:visited
{
display:block;
font-weight:bold;
color:#FFFFFF;
background-color:#98bf21;
width:120px;
text-align:center;
padding:4px;
text-decoration:none;
}
a:hover,a:active
{
background-color:#7A991A;
}
</style>
</head>
<body>
<a href="http://www.google.com" target="_blank">Google Link</a>
</body>
</html>
```

HTML & CSS

Programming Guide

Chapter 21

Background Styles

21. Background Styles

background	It defines all the background properties in one declaration. *Values:* • background-attachment • background-color • background-image • background-position • background-repeat • background-origin • background-break • background-clip • background-size
background-attachment	It defines whether a background image is fixed or scrolls with rest of the page. *Values:* • scroll • fixed
background-color	It defines the background color of an element. *Values:* • color [red, green, blue, etc] • transparent
background-image	It defines the background image of an element. *Values:* • url • none
background-position	It defines the position of the background image. *Values:* • top left • top center • top right • center left • center center

	<ul><li>center right</li><li>bottom left</li><li>bottom right</li><li>x-% y-%</li><li>x-pos y-pos</li></ul>
background-repeat	It defines how a background image will be repeated. *Values:*<ul><li>repeat</li><li>repeat-x</li><li>repeat-y</li><li>no-repeat</li></ul>
background-origin	It defines the origin position of the background image. *Values:*<ul><li>border-box</li><li>padding-box</li><li>content-box</li></ul>
background-break	It defines how the background positioning area is derived from the multiple boxes of attachment. *Values:*<ul><li>bounding-box</li><li>each-box</li><li>continuous</li></ul>
background-clip	It defines whether the background extends into the border area or not. *Values:*<ul><li>border-box</li><li>padding-box</li><li>content-box</li><li>no-clip</li><li>length</li><li>%</li></ul>
background-size	It defines the size of the background image. *Values:*<ul><li>auto</li></ul>

- cover
- contain
- length
- %

Coding Snippets:

Program 21.1
Usage of the background-attachment property

```
<html>
<head>
<title>Usage of background-attachment property</title>
<style>
body
{
background-image:url('sample.gif');
background-repeat:no-repeat;
background-attachment:fixed;
}
</style>
</head>
<body>
<p>Please scroll down the page to see the effect.</p>
<p>The background-image is fixed.</p>
<p>The background-image is fixed.</p>
<p>The background-image is fixed.</p>
<p>The background-image is fixed.</p>
<p>The background-image is fixed.</p>
<p>The background-image is fixed.</p>
<p>The background-image is fixed.</p>
<p>The background-image is fixed.</p>
<p>The background-image is fixed.</p>
<p>The background-image is fixed.</p>
<p>The background-image is fixed.</p>
<p>The background-image is fixed.</p>
<p>The background-image is fixed.</p>
<p>The background-image is fixed.</p>
```

```
<p>The background-image is fixed.</p>
<p>The background-image is fixed.</p>
<p>The background-image is fixed.</p>
<p>The background-image is fixed.</p>
<p>The background-image is fixed.</p>
<p>The background-image is fixed.</p>
<p>The background-image is fixed.</p>
<p>The background-image is fixed.</p>
<p>The background-image is fixed.</p>
<p>The background-image is fixed.</p>
</body>
</html>
```

Program 21.2

Usage of the background-color property

```
<html>
<head>
<title>Usage of background-color property</title>
<style>
body
{
background-color:yellow;
}
h1
{
background-color:#00ff00;
}
p
{
background-color:rgb(255,0,255);
}
</style>
</head>
<body>
<h1>Heading 1 Text.</h1>
<p>Paragraph Text.</p>
</body></html>
```

Program 21.3

Usage of the background-image property

```
<html>
<head>
<title>Usage of background-image property</title>
<style>
body
{
background-image:url('sample.gif');
background-color:#ff0000;
}
</style>
</head>
<body>
<h1>Sample Text</h1>
</body>
</html>
```

Program 21.4

Usage of the background-position property

```
<html>
<head>
<title>Usage of background-position property</title>
<style>
body
{
background-image:url('smiley.gif');
background-repeat:no-repeat;
background-attachment:fixed;
background-position:top;
}
</style>
</head>
<body>
<p>Sample Text.</p>
</body></html>
```

Program 21.5

Usage of the background-position property

```
<html>
<head>
<title>Usage of background-position property</title>
<style>
body
{
background-image:url('smiley.gif');
background-repeat:no-repeat;
background-attachment:fixed;
background-position:top right;
}
</style>
</head>
<body>
<p>Sample Text.</p>
</body>
</html>
```

Program 21.6

Usage of the background-position property

```
<html>
<head>
<title>Usage of background-position property</title>
<style>
body
{
background-image:url('smiley.gif');
background-repeat:no-repeat;
background-attachment:fixed;
background-position:30% 50%;
}
</style>
</head>
<body>
```

```
<p>Sample Text.</p>
</body>
</html>
```

Program 21.7

Usage of the background-position property

```
<html>
<head>
<title>Usage of background-position property</title>
<style>
body
{
background-image:url('smiley.gif');
background-repeat:no-repeat;
background-attachment:fixed;
background-position:58 65;
}
</style>
</head>
<body>
<p>Sample Text.</p>
</body>
</html>
```

HTML & CSS

Programming Guide

Chapter 22

Border Styles

22. Border Styles

border	It defines all the border properties in one declaration. *Values:* • border-color • border-style • border-width • border-radius
border-bottom	It defines all the bottom border properties in one declaration. *Values:* • border-bottom-color • border-bottom-style • border-bottom-width • inherit
border-bottom-color	It defines the color of the bottom border. *Values:* • color • transparent • inherit
border-bottom-style	It defines the style of the bottom border. *Values:* • none • hidden • dotted • dashed • solid • double • groove • ridge • inset • outset • inherit

border-bottom-width	It defines the width of the bottom border. *Values:* • thin • thick • medium • length • inherit
border-color	It defines the color of the four border lines. *Values:* • color • transparent • inherit
border-left	It defines the properties of left border in one declaration. *Values:* • border-left-color • border-left-style • border-left-width
border-left-color	It defines the color of the left border. *Values:* • color • transparent • inherit
border-left-style	It defines the style of the left border. *Values:* • none • hidden • dotted • dashed • solid • double • groove • ridge • inset • outset

	• inherit
border-left-width	It defines the width of the left border. *Values:* • thin • thick • medium • length • inherit
border-right	It defines the properties of right border in one declaration. *Values:* • border-right-color • border-right-style • border-right-width
border-right-color	It defines the color of the right border. *Values:* • color • transparent • inherit
border-right-style	It defines the style of the right border. *Values:* • none • hidden • dotted • dashed • solid • double • groove • ridge • inset • outset • inherit
border-right-width	It defines the width of the right border. *Values:*

	• thin • thick • medium • length • inherit
border-top	It defines the properties of top border in one declaration. *Values:* • border-top-color • border-top-style • border-top-width
border-top-color	It defines the color of the top border. *Values:* • color • transparent • inherit
border-top-style	It defines the style of the top border. *Values:* • none • hidden • dotted • dashed • solid • double • groove • ridge • inset • outset • inherit
border-top-width	It defines the width of the top border. *Values:* • thin • thick • medium • length

	• inherit
border-width	It defines the width of the four border lines. *Values:* • thin • thick • medium • length • inherit
border-radius	It defines the radius of the border corners. *Values:* • border-top-right-radius • border-top-left-radius • border-bottom-right-radius • border-bottom-left-radius
border-top-right-radius	It defines the radius of the top right border corner. *Values:* • length • %
border-top-left-radius	It defines the radius of the top left border corner. *Values:* • length • %
border-bottom-right-radius	It defines the radius of the bottom right border corner. *Values:* • length • %
border-bottom-left-radius	It defines the radius of the bottom left border corner. *Values:* • length • %
border-style	It defines the style of four lines of the border. *Values:* • none

- hidden
- dotted
- dashed
- solid
- double
- groove
- ridge
- inset
- outset
- inherit

Coding Snippets:

Program 22.1

Usage of the border-width property

```
<html>
<head>
<title>Usage of border-width Properties</title>
<style>
p.thin
{
border-style:solid;
border-width:thin;
}
p.medium
{
border-style:solid;
border-width:medium;
}
p.thick
{
border-style:solid;
border-width:thick;
}
p.length
{
```

```
border-style:solid;
border-width:5px;
}
</style>
</head>
<body>
<p class="thin">Sample Text - Border Width Thin.</p>
<p class="medium">Sample Text - Border Width Medium.</p>
<p class="thick">Sample Text - Border Width Thick.</p>
<p class="length">Sample Text - Border Width 5px.</p>
</body>
</html>
```

Program 22.2
Usage of the border-top-width property

```
<html>
<head>
<title>Usage of border-top-width property</title>
<style>
p
{
border-style:solid;
border-top-width:15px;
}
</style>
</head>
<body>
<p>Sample text with top border width 15px.</p>
</body>
</html>
```

Program 22.3
Usage of the border-bottom-width property

```
<html>
<head>
<title>Usage of border-bottom-width property</title>
```

```
<style>
p
{
border-style:solid;
border-bottom-width:15px;
}
</style>
</head>
<body>
<p>Sample text with top border width 15px.</p>
</body>
</html>
```

Program 22.4

Usage of the border-left-width property

```
<html>
<head>
<title>Usage of border-left-width property</title>
<style>
p
{
border-style:solid;
border-left-width:15px;
}
</style>
</head>
<body>
<p>Sample text with left border width 15px.</p>
</body>
</html>
```

Program 22.5

Usage of the border-right-width property

```
<html>
<head>
<title>Usage of border-right-width property</title>
```

```
<style>
p
{
border-style:solid;
border-right-width:15px;
}
</style>
</head>
<body>
<p>Sample text with right border width 15px.</p>
</body>
</html>
```

Program 22.6

Usage of the border-style property

```
<html>
<head>
<title>Usage of border-style Property</title>
<style>
p.none {border-style:none;}
p.dotted {border-style:dotted;}
p.dashed {border-style:dashed;}
p.solid {border-style:solid;}
p.double {border-style:double;}
p.groove {border-style:groove;}
p.ridge {border-style:ridge;}
p.inset {border-style:inset;}
p.outset {border-style:outset;}
p.hidden {border-style:hidden;}
</style>
</head>
<body>
<p class="none">No border.</p>
<p class="dotted">dotted border.</p>
<p class="dashed">dashed border.</p>
<p class="solid">solid border.</p>
<p class="double">double border.</p>
```

```
<p class="groove">groove border.</p>
<p class="ridge">ridge border.</p>
<p class="inset">inset border.</p>
<p class="outset">outset border.</p>
<p class="hidden">hidden border.</p>
</body>
</html>
```

Program 22.7

Usage of the border-top-style property

```
<html>
<head>
<title>Usage of border-top-style property</title>
<style>
p
{
border-style:solid;
}
p.none {border-top-style:none;}
p.dotted {border-top-style:dotted;}
p.dashed {border-top-style:dashed;}
p.solid {border-top-style:solid;}
p.double {border-top-style:double;}
p.groove {border-top-style:groove;}
p.ridge {border-top-style:ridge;}
p.inset {border-top-style:inset;}
p.outset {border-top-style:outset;}
</style>
</head>
<body>
<p class="none">No top border.</p>
<p class="dotted">dotted top border.</p>
<p class="dashed">dashed top border.</p>
<p class="solid">solid top border.</p>
<p class="double">double top border.</p>
<p class="groove">groove top border.</p>
<p class="ridge">ridge top border.</p>
```

```
<p class="inset">inset top border.</p>
<p class="outset">outset top border.</p>
</body>
</html>
```

Program 22.8

Usage of the border-bottom-style property

```
<html>
<head>
<title>Usage of border-bottom-style property</title>
<style>
p {border-style:solid;}
p.none {border-bottom-style:none;}
p.dotted {border-bottom-style:dotted;}
p.dashed {border-bottom-style:dashed;}
p.solid {border-bottom-style:solid;}
p.double {border-bottom-style:double;}
p.groove {border-bottom-style:groove;}
p.ridge {border-bottom-style:ridge;}
p.inset {border-bottom-style:inset;}
p.outset {border-bottom-style:outset;}
</style>
</head>
<body>
<p class="none">No bottom border.</p>
<p class="dotted">dotted bottom border.</p>
<p class="dashed">dashed bottom border.</p>
<p class="solid">solid bottom border.</p>
<p class="double">double bottom border.</p>
<p class="groove">groove bottom border.</p>
<p class="ridge">ridge bottom border.</p>
<p class="inset">inset bottom border.</p>
<p class="outset">outset bottom border.</p>
</body>
</html>
```

Program 22.9

Usage of the border-left-style property

```
<html>
<head>
<title>Usage of border-left-style property</title>
<style>
p
{
border-style:solid;
}
p.none {border-left-style:none;}
p.dotted {border-left-style:dotted;}
p.dashed {border-left-style:dashed;}
p.solid {border-left-style:solid;}
p.double {border-left-style:double;}
p.groove {border-left-style:groove;}
p.ridge {border-left-style:ridge;}
p.inset {border-left-style:inset;}
p.outset {border-left-style:outset;}
</style>
</head>
<body>
<p class="none">No left border.</p>
<p class="dotted">dotted left border.</p>
<p class="dashed">dashed left border.</p>
<p class="solid">solid left border.</p>
<p class="double">double left border.</p>
<p class="groove">groove left border.</p>
<p class="ridge">ridge left border.</p>
<p class="inset">inset left border.</p>
<p class="outset">outset left border.</p>
</body>
</html>
```

Program 22.10

Usage of the border-right-style property

```
<html>
<head>
<title>Usage of border-right-style property</title>
<style>
p
{
border-style:solid;
}
p.none {border-right-style:none;}
p.dotted {border-right-style:dotted;}
p.dashed {border-right-style:dashed;}
p.solid {border-right-style:solid;}
p.double {border-right-style:double;}
p.groove {border-right-style:groove;}
p.ridge {border-right-style:ridge;}
p.inset {border-right-style:inset;}
p.outset {border-right-style:outset;}
</style>
</head>
<body>
<p class="none">No right border.</p>
<p class="dotted">dotted right border.</p>
<p class="dashed">dashed right border.</p>
<p class="solid">solid right border.</p>
<p class="double">double right border.</p>
<p class="groove">groove right border.</p>
<p class="ridge">ridge right border.</p>
<p class="inset">inset right border.</p>
<p class="outset">outset right border.</p>
</body>
</html>
```

Program 22.11

Usage of the border-color property

```
<html>
<head>
<title>Usage of border-color property</title>
<style>
p.one
{
border-style:solid;
border-color:#0000ff;
}
p.two
{
border-style:solid;
border-color:#ff0000 #0000ff;
}
p.three
{
border-style:solid;
border-color:#ff0000 #00ff00 #0000ff;
}
p.four
{
border-style:solid;
border-color:#ff0000 #00ff00 #0000ff rgb(250,0,255);
}
</style>
</head>
<body>
<p class="one">One colored border</p>
<p class="two">Two colored border</p>
<p class="three">Three colored border</p>
<p class="four">Four colored border</p>
</body>
</html>
```

Program 22.12

Usage of the border-top-color property

```
<html>
<head>
<title>Usage of border-top-color property</title>
<style>
p
{
border-style:solid;
border-top-color:#ff0000;
}
</style>
</head>
<body>
<p>Sample text with top border color - #ff0000.</p>
</body>
</html>
```

Program 22.13

Usage of the border-bottom-color property

```
<html>
<head>
<title>Usage of border-bottom-color property</title>
<style>
p
{
border-style:solid;
border-bottom-color:#ff0000;
}
</style>
</head>
<body>
<p>Sample text with bottom border color - #ff0000.</p>
</body>
</html>
```

Program 22.14

Usage of the border-left-color property

```
<html>
<head>
<title>Usage of border-left-color property</title>
<style>
p
{
border-style:solid;
border-left-color:#ff0000;
}
</style>
</head>
<body>
<p>Sample text with left border color - #ff0000.</p>
</body>
</html>
```

Program 22.15

Usage of the border-right-color property

```
<html>
<head>
<title>Usage of border-right-color property</title>
<style>
p
{
border-style:solid;
border-right-color:#ff0000;
}
</style>
</head>
<body>
<p>Sample text with right border color - #ff0000.</p>
</body>
</html>
```

Program 22.16

Usage of the border-radius property

```
<html>
<head>
<title>Usage of border-radius property</title>
<style>
p
{
border-style:solid;
border-radius:5px;
}
</style>
</head>
<body>
<p><br />Sample text with border radius 5px.<br /></p>
</body>
</html>
```

Program 22.17

Usage of the border-top-right-radius property

```
<html>
<head>
<title>Usage of border-top-right-radius property</title>
<style>
p
{
border-style:solid;
border-top-right-radius:5px;
}
</style>
</head>
<body>
<p><br />Sample text with top right border radius 5px.<br /></p>
</body>
</html>
```

Program 22.18

Usage of the border-bottom-right-radius property

```
<html>
<head>
<title>Usage of border-bottom-right-radius property</title>
<style>
p
{
border-style:solid;
border-bottom-right-radius:5px;
}
</style>
</head>
<body>
<p><br />Sample text with bottom right border radius 5px.<br /></p>
</body>
</html>
```

Program 22.19

Usage of the border-top-left-radius property

```
<html>
<head>
<title>Usage of border-top-left-radius property</title>
<style>
p
{
border-style:solid;
border-top-left-radius:5px;
}
</style>
</head>
<body>
<p><br />Sample text with top left border radius 5px.<br /></p>
</body>
</html>
```

Program 22.20

Usage of the border-bottom-left-radius property

```
<html>
<head>
<title>Usage of border-bottom-left-radius property</title>
<style>
p
{
border-style:solid;
border-bottom-left-radius:5px;
}
</style>
</head>
<body>
<p><br />Sample text with bottom left border radius 5px.<br /></p>
</body>
</html>
```

Program 22.21

Usage of the border properties

```
<html>
<head>
<title>Usage of border properties</title>
<style>
p
{
border:5px solid red;
}
</style>
</head>
<body>
<p>
<br />Sample text with border.<br />
</p>
</body>
</html>
```

Program 22.22

Usage of the border-style properties

```
<html>
<head>
<title>Usage of border-style property</title>
<style>
p.one {border-style:dotted solid dashed double;}
p.two {border-style:dotted solid dashed;}
p.three {border-style:dotted solid;}
p.four {border-style:dotted;}
</style>
</head>
<body>
<p class="one">Sample Text 01.</p>
<p class="two">Sample Text 02.</p>
<p class="three">Sample Text 03.</p>
<p class="four">Sample Text 04.</p>
</body>
</html>
```

Program 22.23

Usage of the border-top properties

```
<html>
<head>
<title>Usage of border-top properties</title>
<style>
p
{
border-style:solid;
border-top:thick double #ff0000;
}
</style>
</head>
<body>
<p>Sample text with top border properties.</p>
</body></html>
```

Program 22.24

Usage of the border-bottom properties

```
<html>
<head>
<title>Usage of border-bottom properties</title>
<style>
p
{
border-style:solid;
border-bottom:thick double #ff0000;
}
</style>
</head>
<body>
<p>Sample text with bottom border properties.</p>
</body>
</html>
```

Program 22.25

Usage of the border-right properties

```
<html>
<head>
<title>Usage of border-right properties</title>
<style>
p
{
border-style:solid;
border-right:thick double #ff0000;
}
</style>
</head>
<body>
<p>Sample text with right border properties.</p>
</body>
</html>
```

Program 22.26

Usage of the border-left properties

```
<html>
<head>
<title>Usage of border-left properties</title>
<style>
p
{
border-style:solid;
border-left:thick double #ff0000;
}
</style>
</head>
<body>
<p>Sample text with left border properties.</p>
</body>
</html>
```

HTML & CSS

Programming Guide

Chapter 23

Outline Styles

23. Outline Styles

outline	It defines all the outline properties in one declaration. *Values:* • outline-color • outline-style • outline-width • inherit
outline-color	It defines the color of an outline. *Values:* • color • invert • inherit
outline-style	It defines the style of an outline. *Values:* • none • dotted • dashed • solid • double • groove • ridge • inset • outset • inherit
outline-width	It defines the width of an outline. *Values:* • thin • medium • thick • length • inherit

Coding Snippets:

Program 23.1

Usage of outline property

```
<!DOCTYPE html>
<html>
<head>
<title>Usage of outline property</title>
<style>
p
{
border:1px solid red;
outline:green dotted thick;
}
</style>
</head>
<body>
<p>Paragraph text with outline property.</p>
</body>
</html>
```

Program 23.2

Usage of outline-style property

```
<!DOCTYPE html>
<html>
<head>
<title>Usage of outline-style property</title>
<style>
p.dotted
{
border:1px solid red;
outline-style:dotted;
}
p.dashed
{
border:1px solid red;
```

```
outline-style:dashed;
}
p.solid
{
border:1px solid red;
outline-style:solid;
}
p.double
{
border:1px solid red;
outline-style:double;
}
p.groove
{
border:1px solid red;
outline-style:groove;
}
p.ridge
{
border:1px solid red;
outline-style:ridge;
}
p.inset
{
border:1px solid red;
outline-style:inset;
}
p.outset
{
border:1px solid red;
outline-style:outset;
}
</style>
</head>
<body>
<p class="dotted">Paragraph text with outline-style property -
dotted</p>
```

```
<p class="dashed">Paragraph text with outline-style property -
dashed</p>
<p class="solid">Paragraph text with outline-style property - solid</p>
<p class="double">Paragraph text with outline-style property -
double</p>
<p class="groove">Paragraph text with outline-style property -
groove</p>
<p class="ridge">Paragraph text with outline-style property - ridge</p>
<p class="inset">Paragraph text with outline-style property - inset</p>
<p class="outset">Paragraph text with outline-style property - outset</p>
</body>
</html>
```

Program 23.3

Usage of outline-color property

```
<!DOCTYPE html>
<html>
<head>
<title>Usage of outline-color property</title>
<style>
p
{
border:1px solid red;
outline-style:dotted;
outline-color:#00ff00;
}
</style>
</head>
<body>
<p>Paragraph text with outline-color property</p>
</body>
</html>
```

Program 23.4

Usage of outline-width property

```
<!DOCTYPE html>
```

```
<html>
<head>
<title>Usage of outline-width property</title>
<style>
p.ex1
{
border:1px solid red;
outline-style:solid;
outline-width:thin;
}
p.ex2
{
border:1px solid red;
outline-style:solid;
outline-width:medium;
}
p.ex3
{
border:1px solid red;
outline-style:solid;
outline-width:thick;
}
p.ex4
{
border:1px solid red;
outline-style:solid;
outline-width:5px;
}
</style>
</head>
<body>
<p class="ex1">Paragrpah text with outline-width property - thin</p>
<p class="ex2">Paragrpah text with outline-width property -
medium</p>
<p class="ex3">Paragrpah text with outline-width property - thick</p>
<p class="ex4">Paragrpah text with outline-width - 5px</p>
</body>
</html>
```

HTML & CSS

Programming Guide

Chapter 24

Margin Styles

24. Margin Styles

margin	It defines all the margin properties in one declaration. *Values:* • margin-bottom • margin-left • margin-right • margin-top • inherit
margin-bottom	It defines the bottom margin of an element. *Values:* • auto • length • % • inherit
margin-left	It defines the left margin of an element. *Values:* • auto • length • % • inherit
margin-right	It defines the right margin of an element. *Values:* • auto • length • % • inherit
margin-top	It defines the top margin of an element. *Values:* • auto • length • % • inherit

Coding Snippets:

Program 24.1

Usage of margin property

```
<html>
<head>
<title>Usage of margin property</title>
<style>
p.margin
{
margin-top:50px;
margin-bottom:50px;
margin-right:50px;
margin-left:50px;
}
</style>
</head>
<body>
<p>Paragraph text without margin.</p>
<p class="margin">Paragraph text with margin.</p>
</body>
</html>
```

Program 24.2

Usage of margin-bottom property

```
<html>
<head>
<title>Usage of margin-bottom property</title>
<style>
p.marbottom {margin-bottom:100px}
</style>
</head>
<body>
<p>Paragraph text without margin.</p>
<p class="marbottom">Paragraph text with 100px bottom margin.</p>
<p>Paragraph text without margin.</p>
```

```
</body>
</html>
```

Program 24.3

Usage of margin-top property

```
<html>
<head>
<title>Usage of margin-top property</title>
<style>
p.martop {margin-top:100px}
</style>
</head>
<body>
<p>Paragraph text without margin.</p>
<p class="martop">Paragraph text with 100px top margin.</p>
<p>Paragraph text without margin.</p>
</body>
</html>
```

Program 24.4

Usage of margin-left property

```
<html>
<head>
<title>Usage of margin-left property</title>
<style>
p.marleft {margin-left:100px}
</style>
</head>
<body>
<p>Paragraph text without margin.</p>
<p class="marleft">Paragraph text with 100px left margin.</p>
<p>Paragraph text without margin.</p>
</body>
</html>
```

Program 24.5

Usage of margin-right property

```
<html>
<head>
<title>Usage of margin-right property</title>
<style>
p.marright {margin-right:100px}
</style>
</head>
<body>
<p>Paragraph text without margin. Paragraph text without margin. Paragraph text without margin. Paragraph text without margin.</p>
<p class="marright">Paragraph text with 100px right margin. Paragraph text with 100px right margin. Paragraph text with 100px right margin. Paragraph text with 100px right margin. Paragraph text with 100px right margin.</p>
<p>Paragraph text without margin. Paragraph text without margin. Paragraph text without margin. Paragraph text without margin. Paragraph text without margin.</p>
</body>
</html>
```

HTML & CSS

Programming Guide

Chapter 25

Padding Styles

25. Padding Styles

padding	It defines all the padding properties in one declaration. *Values:* • padding-bottom • padding-left • padding-right • padding-top • inherit
padding-bottom	It defines the bottom padding of an element. *Values:* • length • % • inherit
padding-left	It defines the left padding of an element. *Values:* • length • % • Inherit
padding-right	It defines the right padding of an element. *Values:* • length • % • Inherit
padding-top	It defines the top padding of an element. *Values:* • length • % • inherit

Coding Snippets:

Program 25.1
Usage of padding property

```
<html>
<head>
<title>Usage of padding property</title>
<style>
p
{
background-color:#00ff00;
}
p.padding
{
padding-top:15px;
padding-bottom:15px;
padding-right:30px;
padding-left:30px;
}
</style>
</head>
<body>
<p>Paragraph text with no padding.</p>
<p class="padding">Paragraph text with padding spaces.</p>
</body>
</html>
```

Program 25.2
Usage of padding-bottom property

```
<html>
<head>
<title>Usage of padding-bottom property</title>
<style>
p
{
background-color:#00ff00;
```

```
}
p.ex1
{
padding-bottom:15px;
}
</style>
</head>
<body>
<p>Paragraph text with no padding.</p>
<p class="ex1">Paragraph text with bottom padding spaces.</p>
</body>
</html>
```

Program 25.3

Usage of padding-top property

```
<html>
<head>
<title>Usage of padding-top property</title>
<style>
p
{
background-color:#00ff00;
}
p.ex1
{
padding-top:15px;
}
</style>
</head>
<body>
<p>Paragraph text with no padding.</p>
<p class="ex1">Paragraph text with top padding spaces.</p>
</body>
</html>
```

Program 25.4

Usage of padding-left property

```html
<html>
<head>
<title>Usage of padding-left property</title>
<style>
p
{
background-color:#00ff00;
}
p.ex1
{
padding-left:35px;
}
</style>
</head>
<body>
<p>Paragraph text with no padding.</p>
<p class="ex1">Paragraph text with left padding spaces.</p>
</body>
</html>
```

Program 25.5

Usage of padding-right property

```html
<html>
<head>
<title>Usage of padding-right property</title>
<style>
p
{
background-color:#00ff00;
}
p.ex1
{
padding-right:125px;
}
```

```
</style>
</head>
<body>
<p>Paragraph text with no padding. Paragraph text with no padding.
Paragraph text with no padding. Paragraph text with no padding.
Paragraph text with no padding.</p>
<p class="ex1">Paragraph text with right padding spaces. Paragraph text
with right padding spaces. Paragraph text with right padding spaces.
Paragraph text with right padding spaces.</p>
<p>Paragraph text with no padding. Paragraph text with no padding.
Paragraph text with no padding. Paragraph text with no padding.
Paragraph text with no padding.</p>
</body>
</html>
```

HTML & CSS

Programming Guide

Chapter 26

Dimension Styles

26. Dimension Styles

height	It defines the height of an element. *Values:* • auto • length • % • inherit
max-height	It defines the maximum height of an element. *Values:* • none • length • % • inherit
min-height	It defines the minimum height of an element. *Values:* • length • % • inherit
width	It defines the width of an element. *Values:* • auto • length • % • inherit
max-width	It defines the maximum width of an element. *Values:* • none • length • % • Inherit
min-width	It defines the minimum width of an element. *Values:*

- length
- %
- inherit

Coding Snippets:

Program 26.1
Usage of height property

```
<html>
<head>
<title>Usage of height property</title>
<style>
img.ex1
{
height:auto;
}
img.ex2
{
height:100px;
}
img.ex2
{
height:200px;
}
</style>
</head>
<body>
<img class="ex1" src="sample.jpg" />
<img class="ex2" src="sample.jpg" />
<img class="ex3" src="sample.jpg" />
</body>
</html>
```

Program 26.2
Usage of width property

```
<html>
```

```
<head>
<title>Usage of width property</title>
<style>
img.ex1
{
width:auto;
}
img.ex2
{
width:50%;
}
img.ex2
{
width:200px;
}
</style>
</head>
<body>
<img class="ex1" src="sample.jpg" />
<img class="ex2" src="sample.jpg" />
<img class="ex3" src="sample.jpg" />
</body>
</html>
```

Program 26.3

Usage of max-height property

```
<html>
<head>
<title>Usage of max-height property</title>
<style>
p
{
max-height:50px;
background-color:yellow;
}
</style>
</head>
```

```
<body>
<p>Paragraph text with maximum height 50px. Paragraph text with
maximum height 50px. Paragraph text with maximum height 50px.
Paragraph text with maximum height 50px. Paragraph text with
maximum height 50px. Paragraph text with maximum height 50px.
Paragraph text with maximum height 50px. Paragraph text with
maximum height 50px. Paragraph text with maximum height 50px. </p>
</body>
</html>
```

Program 26.4

Usage of max-width property

```
<!DOCTYPE html>
<html>
<head>
<style>
p
{
max-width:100px;
background-color:yellow;
}
</style>
</head>
<body>
<p>The maximum width of this paragraph is set to 100px. The maximum
width of this paragraph is set to 100px.</p>
</body>
</html>
```

Program 26.5

Usage of min-height property

```
<!DOCTYPE html>
<html>
<head>
<style>
```

```
p
{
min-height:100px;
background-color:yellow;
}
</style>
</head>
<body>
<p>Paragraph text with minimum height 100px.</p>
</body>
</html>
```

Program 26.6

Usage of min-width property

```
<!DOCTYPE html>
<html>
<head>
<title>Usage of min-width property</title>
<style>
p
{
min-width:50px;
background-color:yellow;
}
</style>
</head>
<body>
<p>Paragraph text with minimum width 150px.</p>
</body>
</html>
```

HTML & CSS

Programming Guide

Chapter 27

Box Styles

27. Box Styles

overflow	It defines whether or not to clip the edges of the content, if it overflows the element's content area. *Values:* • visible • hidden • scroll • auto • no-display • no-content • overflow-x • overflow-y
overflow-x	It defines whether or not to clip the right/left edges of the content, if it overflows the element's content area. *Values:* • visible • hidden • scroll • auto • no-display • no-content
overflow-y	It defines whether or not to clip the top/bottom edges of the content, if it overflows the element's content area. *Values:* • visible • hidden • scroll • auto • no-display • no-content
overflow-style	It defines the overflow of style of the content.

	Values: • auto • marquee-line • marquee-block
rotation	It rotates an element around a given point defined by the rotation-point property. *Values:* • angle
rotation-point	It defines a point as an offset from the top left border edge. *Values:* • position (paired value off-set)
visibility	It defines the visibility of the content block or an element. *Values:* • visible • hidden • collapse

Coding Snippets:

Program 27.1

Usage of overflow property

```
<html>
<head>
<title>Usage of overflow property</title>
<style>
div.scroll
{
background-color:#00FFFF;
width:100px;
height:100px;
overflow:scroll;
}
div.hidden
```

```
{
background-color:#00FF00;
width:100px;
height:100px;
overflow:hidden;
}
div.visible
{
background-color:#00FF00;
width:100px;
height:100px;
overflow:visible;
}
div.auto
{
background-color:#00FF00;
width:100px;
height:100px;
overflow:auto;
}
div.nodisplay
{
background-color:#00FF00;
width:100px;
height:100px;
overflow:no-display;
}
div.nocontent
{
background-color:#00FF00;
width:100px;
height:100px;
overflow:no content;
}
</style>
</head>
<body>
<p></p>
```

```
<p>overflow property with scrol value</p>
<div class="scroll">Sample text with overflow property. Sample text with
overflow property. Sample text with overflow property.</div>
<p>overflow property with hidden value</p>
<div class="hidden">Sample text with overflow property. Sample text with
overflow property. Sample text with overflow property.</div>
<p>overflow property with visible value</p>
<div class="visible">Sample text with overflow property. Sample text with
overflow property. Sample text with overflow property.</div>
<p>overflow property with auto value</p>
<div class="auto">Sample text with overflow property. Sample text with
overflow property. Sample text with overflow property.</div>
<p>overflow property with no-display value</p>
<div class="nodisplay">Sample text with overflow property. Sample text
with overflow property. Sample text with overflow property.</div>
<p>overflow property with no-content value</p>
<div class="nocontent">Sample text with overflow property. Sample text
with overflow property. Sample text with overflow property.</div>
</body>
</html>
```

Program 27.2

Usage of overflow-x & overflow-y property

```
<html>
<head>
<title>Usage of overflow-x & overflow-y property</title>
<style>
div
{
width:110px;
height:110px;
border:thin solid black;
overflow-x:hidden;
overflow-y:hidden;
}
</style>
</head>
```

```
<body>
<div><p style="width:110px">
Sample paragraph text with overflow property. Sample paragraph text
with overflow property. Sample paragraph text with overflow property.
Sample paragraph text with overflow property.
</p></div>
</body>
</html>
```

Program 27.3

Usage of overflow-x & overflow-y property

```
<html>
<head>
<title>Usage of visibility property</title>
<style>
p.visible {visibility:visible}
p.hidden {visibility:hidden}
</style>
</head>
<body>
<p class="visible">This is visible paragraph text.</h1>
<p class="hidden">This is invisible paragraph text.</h1>
<p>This is normal paragraph text.</p>
</body>
</html>
```

HTML & CSS

Programming Guide

Chapter 28

Position Styles

28. Position Styles

bottom	It defines the bottom margin edge for a positioned box. *Values:* • auto • length • % • inherit
clip	It clips an absolutely positioned element. *Values:* • auto • shape • inherit
cursor	It defines the type of cursor to be displayed. *Values:* • url • auto • crosshair • default • pointer • move • e-resize • ne-resize • nw-resize • n-resize • se-resize • sw-resize • s-resize • w-resize • text • wait • help
left	It defines the left margin edge for a positioned box.

	Values: • auto • length • % • inherit
position	It defines the type of positioning for an element. *Values:* • absolute • fixed • relative • static • inherit
right	It defines the right margin edge for a positioned box. *Values:* • auto • length • % • inherit
top	It defines the top margin edge for a positioned box. *Values:* • auto • length • % • inherit
z-index	It defines the stack order of an element. *Values:* • number • auto • inherit

Coding Snippets:

Program 28.1

Usage of bottom property

```
<html>
<head>
<title>Usage of bottom property</title>
<style>
img.ex1
{
position:absolute;
bottom:0px;
}
img.ex2
{
position:relative;
bottom:-100px;
}
</style>
</head>
<body>
<img class="ex1" src="sample.jpg">
<h1>Heading Text.</h1>
<img class="ex2" src="sample.jpg">
</body>
</html>
```

Program 28.2

Usage of clip property

```
<html>
<head>
<title>Usage of clip property</title>
<style>
img
{
position:absolute;
```

```
clip:rect(0px,50px,150px,0px);
}
</style>
</head>
<body>
<img src="sample.jpg" />
</body>
</html>
```

Program 28.3

Usage of cursor property

```
<html>
<head>
<title>Usage of cursor property</title>
<style>
p.auto
{
cursor:auto;
}
p.crosshair
{
cursor:crosshair;
}
p.default
{
cursor:default;
}
p.pointer
{
cursor:pointer;
}
p.move
{
cursor:move;
}
p.eresize
{
```

```
cursor:e-resize;
}
p.neresize
{
cursor:ne-resize;
}
p.nwresize
{
cursor:nw-resize;
}
p.nresize
{
cursor:n-resize;
}
p.seresize
{
cursor:se-resize;
}
p.swresize
{
cursor:sw-resize;
}
p.sresize
{
cursor:s-resize;
}
p.wresize
{
cursor:w-resize;
}
p.text
{
cursor:text;
}
p.wait
{
cursor:wait;
}
```

```
</style>
</head>
<body>
<p class="auto">Paragraph Text with Cursor Type : auto</p>
<p class="crosshair">Paragraph Text with Cursor Type : crosshair</p>
<p class="default">Paragraph Text with Cursor Type : default</p>
<p class="pointer">Paragraph Text with Cursor Type : pointer</p>
<p class="move">Paragraph Text with Cursor Type : move</p>
<p class="eresize">Paragraph Text with Cursor Type : e-resize</p>
<p class="neresize">Paragraph Text with Cursor Type : ne-resize</p>
<p class="nwresize">Paragraph Text with Cursor Type : nw-resize</p>
<p class="nresize">Paragraph Text with Cursor Type : n-resize</p>
<p class="seresize">Paragraph Text with Cursor Type : se-resize</p>
<p class="swresize">Paragraph Text with Cursor Type : sw-resize</p>
<p class="sresize">Paragraph Text with Cursor Type : s-resize</p>
<p class="wresize">Paragraph Text with Cursor Type : w-resize</p>
<p class="text">Paragraph Text with Cursor Type : text</p>
<p class="wait">Paragraph Text with Cursor Type : wait</p>
</body>
</html>
```

Program 28.4

Usage of left property

```
<html>
<head>
<title>Usage of left property</title>
<style>
img
{
position:absolute;
left:50px;
}
</style>
</head>
<body>
<p>This is a paragraph text</p>
<img src="sample.jpg" />
```

```
</body>
</html>
```

Program 28.5

Usage of right property

```
<html>
<head>
<title>Usage of right property</title>
<style>
img
{
position:absolute;
right:50px;
}
</style>
</head>
<body>
<p>This is a paragraph text</p>
<img src="sample.jpg" />
</body>
</html>
```

Program 28.6

Usage of top property

```
<html>
<head>
<title>Usage of top property</title>
<style>
img
{
position:absolute;
top:0px;
}
</style>
</head>
<body>
```

```
<p>This is a paragraph text</p>
<img src="sample.jpg" />
</body>
</html>
```

Program 28.7

Usage of z-index property

```
<html>
<head>
<title>Usage of z-index property</title>
<style>
img
{
position:absolute;
left:0px;
top:0px;
z-index:-1;
}
</style>
</head>
<body>
<h1>This is a heading text.</h1>
<img src="sample.jpg" />
<p>This is a paragraph text.</p>
</body>
</html>
```

Program 28.8

Usage of position property

```
<html>
<head>
<title>Usage of position property</title>
<style>
h1
{
position:absolute;
```

```
left:150px;
top:150px;
}
</style>
</head>
<body>
<h1>This is a heading text.</h1>
<p>This is a paragraph text. This is a paragraph text. This is a paragraph text. This is a paragraph text. This is a paragraph text. This is a paragraph text.</p>
</body>
</html>
```

Program 28.9

Usage of position property

```
<html>
<head>
<title>Usage of position property</title>
<style>
h1
{
position:relative;
left:150px;
top:150px;
}
</style>
</head>
<body>
<h1>This is a heading text.</h1>
<p>This is a paragraph text. This is a paragraph text. This is a paragraph text. This is a paragraph text. This is a paragraph text. This is a paragraph text.</p>
</body>
</html>
```

HTML & CSS

Programming Guide

Chapter 29

Floating Styles

29. Floating Styles

clear	It defines which sides of an element where other floating elements are not allowed. *Values:* • left • right • both • none • inherit
float	It defines whether or not a box should float. *Values:* • left • right • none • inherit

Coding Snippets:

Program 29.1

Usage of float property

```
<html>
<head>
<title>Usage of float property</title>
<style>
img
{
float:left;
}
</style>
</head>
<body>
<img src="sample.jpg" width="100" height="100" />
```

```
<p>This is a paragraph text. This is a paragraph text. This is a paragraph
text. This is a paragraph text. This is a paragraph text. This is a
paragraph text. This is a paragraph text. </p>
</body>
</html>
```

Program 29.2

Usage of clear property

```
<html>
<head>
<title>Usage of float & clear property</title>
<style>
img
{
float:left;
}
p.ex1
{
clear:both;
}
</style>
</head>
<body>
<img src="sample.jpg" width="100" height="100" />
<p>This is a paragraph text. This is a paragraph text. This is a paragraph
text. This is a paragraph text. This is a paragraph text. This is a
paragraph text. This is a paragraph text. </p>
<p class="ex1">This is a paragraph text. This is a paragraph text. This is
a paragraph text. This is a paragraph text. This is a paragraph text. This
is a paragraph text. This is a paragraph text. </p>
</body>
</html>
```

Program 29.3

Usage of float & clear property

```html
<html>
<head>
<title>Usage of float & clear property</title>
<style>
img
{
float:left;
}
p.ex1
{
clear:left;
}
</style>
</head>
<body>
<img src="sample.jpg" width="100" height="100" />
<p>This is a paragraph text. This is a paragraph text. This is a paragraph
text. This is a paragraph text. This is a paragraph text. This is a
paragraph text. This is a paragraph text. </p>
<p class="ex1">This is a paragraph text. This is a paragraph text. This is
a paragraph text. This is a paragraph text. This is a paragraph text. This
is a paragraph text. This is a paragraph text. </p>
</body>
</html>
```

HTML & CSS

Programming Guide

Chapter 30

Marquee Styles

30. Marquee Styles

marquee	It defines the marquee properties of moving content. *Values:* • marquee-direction • marquee-play-count • marquee-speed • marquee-style
direction	It defines the direction of the moving content. *Values:* • left • right • up • down
behavior	It defines the behavior of the moving content. *Values:* • scroll • slide • alternate
loop	It defines the number of the loops. *Values:* • number
scrolldelay	It defines the scrolling delay of moving text. *Values:* • number (milliseconds)
scrollamount	It defines the amount of movement. *Values:* • pixels

Coding Snippets:

Program 30.1

Usage of marquee property

```
<html>
<head>
<title>Usage of marquee property</title>
<style>
</style>
</head>
<body>
<marquee>Moving text with marquee tag.</marquee>
</body>
</html>
```

Program 30.2

Usage of direction property

```
<html>
<head>
<title>Usage of direction property</title>
<style>
</style>
</head>
<body>
<marquee direction="right">Moving text with marquee tag - right
direction</marquee>
</body>
</html>
```

Program 30.3

Usage of direction property

```
<html>
<head>
<title>Usage of direction property</title>
<style>
```

```
</style>
</head>
<body>
<marquee direction="up">Moving text with marquee tag - up
direction.</marquee>
</body>
</html>
```

Program 30.4

Usage of behavior property

```
<html>
<head>
<title>Usage of behavior property</title>
<style>
</style>
</head>
<body>
<marquee direction="left" behavior="alternate"> Moving text with
marquee tag.</marquee>
</body>
</html>
```

Program 30.5

Usage of behavior property

```
<html>
<head>
<title>Usage of behavior property</title>
<style>
</style>
</head>
<body>
<marquee direction="left" behavior="slide"> Moving text with marquee
tag.</marquee>
</body>
</html>
```

Program 30.6

Usage of loop property

```
<html>
<head>
<title>Usage of behavior property</title>
<style>
</style>
</head>
<body>
<marquee direction="left" behavior="scroll" loop="2"> Moving text with
marquee tag.</marquee>
</body>
</html>
```

Program 30.7

Usage of scrolldelay property

```
<html>
<head>
<title>Usage of scrolldelay property</title>
<style>
</style>
</head>
<body>
<marquee direction="left" behavior="scroll" loop="2" scrolldelay="3">
Moving text with marquee tag.</marquee>
</body>
</html>
```

Program 30.8

Usage of scrollamount property

```
<html>
<head>
<title>Usage of scrollamount property</title>
<style>
</style>
```

```
</head>
<body>
<marquee direction="left" behavior="scroll" loop="2" scrolldelay="3"
scrollamount="400px"> Moving text with marquee tag.</marquee>
</body>
</html>
```

HTML & CSS

Programming Guide

Chapter 31

Color Styles

31. Color Styles

color	It defines the color of an element. *Values:* • color • inherit
opacity	It defines opacity of an element. *Values:* • number • inherit

Coding Snippets:

Program 31.1

Usage of color property

```
<html>
<head>
<style>Usage of color property</style>
<style>
p
{
color:red;
}
</style>
</head>
<body>
<p>Paragraph text with red color font.</p>
</body>
</html>
```

Program 31.2

Usage of opacity property

```
<!DOCTYPE html>
<html>
```

```
<head>
<title>Usage of opacity property</title>
<style>
p
{
background-color:red;
opacity:0.5;
filter:Alpha(opacity=50);
}
</style>
</head>
<body>
<p>Paragraph text with opacity 0.5.</p>
</body>
</html>
```

Program 31.3

Usage of background-color property

```
<html>
<head>
<style>Usage of color property</style>
<style>
body
{
background-color:red;
}
</style>
</head>
<body>
<p>Paragraph text with red color background.</p>
</body>
</html>
```

PART - III

HTML & CSS

Reference

HTML & CSS

Programming Guide

Appendix 01

Color Names & Hex Values

01. Color Names & Hex Values

Color Name	Hex Values	Color Name	Hex Values
aliceblue	#f0f8ff	darkcyan	#008b8b
antiquewhite	#faebd7	darkgoldenrod	#b8860b
aqua	#00ffff	darkgray	#a9a9a9
aquamarine	#7fffd4	darkgreen	#640000
azure	#f0ffff	darkkhaki	#bdb76b
beige	#f5f5dc	darkmagenta	#8b008b
bisque	#ffe4c4	darkolivegreen	#556b2f
black	#000000	darkorange	#ff8b04
blanchedalmond	#ffebcd	darkorchid	#9932cc
blue	#0000ff	darkred	#8b0000
blueviolet	#8a2be2	darksalmon	#e9967a
brown	#a52a2a	darkseagreen	#8fbc8f
burlywood	#deb887	darkslateblue	#483d8b
cadetblue	#5f9ea0	darkslategray	#2f4f4f
chartreuse	#7fff00	darkturquoise	#00ced1
chocolate	#d2691e	darkviolet	#9400d3
coral	#ff7f50	deeppink	#ff1493
cornflowerblue	#6495ed	deepskyblue	#00bfff
cornsilk	#fff8dc	dimgray	#696969
crimson	#dc143c	dodgerblue	#1e90ff
cyan	#00ffff	firebrick	#b22222
darkblue	#00008b	floralwhite	#fffaf0

forestgreen	#228b22	lightpink	#ffb6c1
fuchsia	#ff00ff	lightsalmon	#ffa07a
gainsboro	#dcdcdc	lightseagreen	#20b2aa
ghostwhite	#f8f8ff	lightskyblue	#87cefa
gold	#ffd700	lightslategray	#778899
goldenrod	#daa520	lightsteelblue	#b0c4de
gray	#808080	lightyellow	#ffffe0
green	#800000	lime	#00ff00
greenyellow	#adff2f	limegreen	#32cd32
honeydew	#f0fff0	linen	#faf0e6
hotpink	#ff69b4	magenta	#ff00ff
indianred	#cd5c5c	maroon	#800000
indigo	#4b0082	mediumaquamarine	#66cdaa
ivory	#fffff0	mediumblue	#0000cd
khaki	#f0e68c	mediumorchid	#ba55d3
lavender	#e6e6fa	mediumpurple	#9370db
lavenderblush	#fff0f5	mediumseagreen	#3cb371
lawngreen	#7cfb04	mediumslateblue	#7b68ee
lemonchiffon	#fffacd	mediumspringgreen	#00fa9a
lightblue	#add8e6	mediumturquoise	#48d1cc
lightcoral	#f08080	mediumvioletred	#c71585
lightcyan	#e0ffff	midnightblue	#191970
lightgoldenrodyellow	#fafad2	mintcream	#f5fffa
lightgreen	#90ee90	mistyrose	#ffe4e1
lightgrey	#d3d3d3	moccasin	#ffe4b5

navajowhite	#ffdead	salmon	#fa8072
navy	#800000	sandybrown	#f4a460
oldlace	#fdf5e6	seagreen	#2e8b57
olive	#808000	seashell	#fff5ee
olivedrab	#6b8e23	sienna	#a0522d
orange	#ffa500	silver	#c0c0c0
orangered	#ff4500	skyblue	#87ceeb
orchid	#da70d6	slateblue	#6a5acd
palegoldenrod	#eee8aa	slategray	#708090
palegreen	#98fb98	snow	#fffafa
paleturquoise	#afeeee	springgreen	#00ff7f
palevioletred	#db7093	steelblue	#4682b4
papayawhip	#ffefd5	tan	#d2b48c
peachpuff	#ffdab9	teal	#808000
peru	#cd853f	thistle	#d8bfd8
pink	#ffc0cb	tomato	#ff6347
plum	#dda0dd	turquoise	#40e0d0
powderblue	#b0e0e6	violet	#ee82ee
purple	#800080	wheat	#f5deb3
red	#ff0000	white	#ffffff
rosybrown	#bc8f8f	whitesmoke	#f5f5f5
royalblue	#416900	yellow	#ffff00
saddlebrown	#8b4513	yellowgreen	#9acd32

HTML & CSS

Programming Guide

Appendix 02

Character Set Types

02. Character Set Types

Character set	Description	Covers
ISO-8859-1	Latin alphabet part 1	North America, Western Europe, Latin America, the Caribbean, Canada, Africa
ISO-8859-2	Latin alphabet part 2	Eastern Europe
ISO-8859-3	Latin alphabet part 3	SE Europe, Esperanto, miscellaneous others
ISO-8859-4	Latin alphabet part 4	Scandinavia/Baltics (and others not in ISO-8859-1)
ISO-8859-5	Latin/Cyrillic part 5	The languages that are using a Cyrillic alphabet such as Bulgarian, Belarusian, Russian and Macedonian
ISO-8859-6	Latin/Arabic part 6	The languages that are using the Arabic alphabet
ISO-8859-7	Latin/Greek part 7	The modern Greek language as well as mathematical symbols derived from the Greek
ISO-8859-8	Latin/Hebrew part 8	The languages that are using the Hebrew alphabet
ISO-8859-9	Latin 5 part 9	The Turkish language. Same as ISO-8859-1 except Turkish characters replace Icelandic ones
ISO-8859-10	Latin 6 Lappish, Nordic, Eskimo	The Nordic languages
ISO-8859-15	Latin 9 (aka Latin 0)	Similar to ISO 8859-1 but replaces some less common symbols with the euro sign and some other missing characters
ISO-2022-JP	Latin/Japanese part 1	The Japanese language
ISO-2022-JP-2	Latin/Japanese part 2	The Japanese language
ISO-2022-KR	Latin/Korean part 1	The Korean language

HTML & CSS

Programming Guide

Appendix 03

ASCII
Character Set

03. ASCII Character Set

Device Controlled Characters

ASCII Character	HTML Entity Code	URL Encoding
NUL	&#00;	%00
SOH	&#01;	%01
STX	&#02;	%02
ETX	&#03;	%03
EOT	&#04;	%04
ENQ	&#05;	%05
ACK	&#06;	%06
BEL	&#07;	%07
BS	&#08;	%08
HT	&#09;	%09
LF	&#10;	%0A
VT	&#11;	%0B
FF	&#12;	%0C
CR	&#13;	%0D
SO	&#14;	%0E
SI	&#15;	%0F
DLE	&#16;	%10
DC1	&#17;	%11
DC2	&#18;	%12
DC3	&#19;	%13

DC4	&#20;	%14
NAK	&#21;	%15
SYN	&#22;	%16
ETB	&#23;	%17
CAN	&#24;	%18
EM	&#25;	%19
SUB	&#26;	%1A
ESC	&#27;	%1B
FS	&#28;	%1C
GS	&#29;	%1D
RS	&#30;	%1E
US	&#31;	%1F
DEL	&#127;	%7F

Printable Characters

ASCII Character	HTML Entity Code	URL Encoding
Space	 	%20
!	!	%21
"	"	%22
#	#	%23
$	$	%24
%	%	%25
&	&	%26
'	'	%27

(	&#40;	%28
)	&#41;	%29
*	&#42;	%2A
+	&#43;	%2B
,	&#44;	%2C
-	&#45;	%2D
.	&#46;	%2E
/	&#47;	%2F
0	&#48;	%30
1	&#49;	%31
2	&#50;	%32
3	&#51;	%33
4	&#52;	%34
5	&#53;	%35
6	&#54;	%36
7	&#55;	%37
8	&#56;	%38
9	&#57;	%39
:	&#58;	%3A
;	&#59;	%3B
<	&#60;	%3C
=	&#61;	%3D
>	&#62;	%3E
?	&#63;	%3F
@	&#64;	%40

A	&#65;	%41
B	&#66;	%42
C	&#67;	%43
D	&#68;	%44
E	&#69;	%45
F	&#70;	%46
G	&#71;	%47
H	&#72;	%48
I	&#73;	%49
J	&#74;	%4A
K	&#75;	%4B
L	&#76;	%4C
M	&#77;	%4D
N	&#78;	%4E
O	&#79;	%4F
P	&#80;	%50
Q	&#81;	%51
R	&#82;	%52
S	&#83;	%53
T	&#84;	%54
U	&#85;	%55
V	&#86;	%56
W	&#87;	%57
X	&#88;	%58
Y	&#89;	%59

Z	&#90;	%5A
[	&#91;	%5B
\	&#92;	%5C
]	&#93;	%5D
^	&#94;	%5E
_	&#95;	%5F
`	&#96;	%60
a	&#97;	%61
b	&#98;	%62
c	&#99;	%63
d	&#100;	%64
e	&#101;	%65
f	&#102;	%66
g	&#103;	%67
h	&#104;	%68
i	&#105;	%69
j	&#106;	%6A
k	&#107;	%6B
l	&#108;	%6C
m	&#109;	%6D
n	&#110;	%6E
o	&#111;	%6F
p	&#112;	%70
q	&#113;	%71
r	&#114;	%72

s	&#115;	%73
t	&#116;	%74
u	&#117;	%75
v	&#118;	%76
w	&#119;	%77
x	&#120;	%78
y	&#121;	%79
z	&#122;	%7A
{	&#123;	%7B
|	|	%7C
}	&#125;	%7D
~	&#126;	%7E

HTML & CSS

Programming Guide

Appendix 04

ISO
Character Set

04. ISO Character Set

Symbols

ASCII Character	HTML Entity Code	URL Encoding
Non-breaking space		%A0
¡	&#161;	%A1
¢	&#162;	%A2
£	&#163;	%A3
€	&#164;	%A4
¥	&#165;	%A5
¦	&#166;	%A6
§	&#167;	%A7
¨	&#168;	%A8
©	&#169;	%A9
ª	&#170;	%AA
«	&#171;	%AB
¬	&#172;	%AC
Soft hyphen	&#173;	%AD
®	&#174;	%AE
¯	&#175;	%AF
°	&#176;	%B0
±	&#177;	%B1
2	&#178;	%B2
3	&#179;	%B3

	&#180;	%B4
μ	&#181;	%B5
¶	&#182;	%B6
·	&#183;	%B7
¸	&#184;	%B8
1	&#185;	%B9
º	&#186;	%BA
»	&#187;	%BB
¼	&#188;	%BC
½	&#189;	%BD
¾	&#190;	%BE
¿	&#191;	%BF

Characters

ASCII Character	HTML Entity Code	URL Encoding
À	&#192;	%C0
Á	&#193;	%C1
Â	&#194;	%C2
Ã	&#195;	%C3
Ä	&#196;	%C4
Å	&#197;	%C5
Æ	&#198;	%C6
Ç	&#199;	%C7
È	&#200;	%C8

É	É	%C9
Ê	Ê	%CA
Ë	Ë	%CB
Ì	Ì	%CC
Í	Í	%CD
Î	Î	%CE
Ï	Ï	%CF
Ð	Ð	%D0
Ñ	Ñ	%D1
Ò	Ò	%D2
Ó	Ó	%D3
Ô	Ô	%D4
Õ	Õ	%D5
Ö	Ö	%D6
×	×	%D7
Ø	Ø	%D8
Ù	Ù	%D9
Ú	Ú	%DA
Û	Û	%DB
Ü	Ü	%DC
Ý	Ý	%DD
Þ	Þ	%DE
ß	ß	%DF
à	à	%E0
á	á	%E1

â	â	%E2
ã	ã	%E3
ä	ä	%E4
å	å	%E5
æ	æ	%E6
ç	ç	%E7
è	è	%E8
é	é	%E9
ê	ê	%EA
ë	ë	%EB
ì	ì	%EC
í	í	%ED
î	î	%EE
ï	ï	%EF
ð	ð	%F0
ñ	ñ	%F1
ò	ò	%F2
ó	ó	%F3
ô	ô	%F4
õ	õ	%F5
ö	ö	%F6
÷	÷	%F7
ø	ø	%F8
ù	ù	%F9
ú	ú	%FA

û	û	%FB
ü	ü	%FC
ý	ý	%FD
þ	þ	%FE
ÿ	ÿ	%FF

HTML & CSS

Programming Guide

Appendix 05

Symbol Entities

05. Symbol Entities

Mathematical Symbols

Symbol	Entity Code	Entity Name	Description
∀	∀	∀	for all
∂	∂	∂	part
∃	∃	∃	exists
∅	∅	∅	empty
∇	∇	∇	nabla
∈	∈	∈	isin
∉	∉	∉	notin
∋	∋	∋	ni
∏	∏	∏	prod
∑	∑	∑	sum
−	−	−	minus
∗	∗	∗	lowast
√	√	√	square root
∝	∝	∝	proportional to
∞	∞	∞	infinity
∠	∠	∠	angle
∧	∧	∧	and
∨	∨	∨	or
∩	∩	∩	cap
∪	∪	∪	cup

∫	∫	∫	integral
∴	∴	∴	therefore
~	∼	∼	similar to
≅	≅	≅	congruent to
≈	≈	≈	almost equal
≠	≠	≠	not equal
≡	≡	≡	equivalent
≤	≤	≤	less or equal
≥	≥	≥	greater or equal
⊂	⊂	⊂	subset of
⊃	⊃	⊃	superset of
⊄	⊄	⊄	not subset of
⊆	⊆	⊆	subset or equal
⊇	⊇	⊇	superset or equal
⊕	⊕	⊕	circled plus
⊗	⊗	⊗	circled times
⊥	⊥	⊥	perpendicular
·	⋅	⋅	dot operator

Greek Letters

Symbol	Entity Code	Entity Name	Description
Α	Α	Α	Alpha
Β	Β	Β	Beta
Γ	Γ	Γ	Gamma

Δ	&#916;	&Delta;	Delta
E	&#917;	&Epsilon;	Epsilon
Z	&#918;	&Zeta;	Zeta
H	&#919;	&Eta;	Eta
Θ	&#920;	&Theta;	Theta
I	&#921;	&Iota;	Iota
K	&#922;	&Kappa;	Kappa
Λ	&#923;	&Lambda;	Lambda
M	&#924;	&Mu;	Mu
N	&#925;	&Nu;	Nu
Ξ	&#926;	&Xi;	Xi
O	&#927;	&Omicron;	Omicron
Π	&#928;	&Pi;	Pi
P	&#929;	&Rho;	Rho
Σ	&#931;	&Sigma;	Sigma
T	&#932;	&Tau;	Tau
Υ	&#933;	&Upsilon;	Upsilon
Φ	&#934;	&Phi;	Phi
X	&#935;	&Chi;	Chi
Ψ	&#936;	&Psi;	Psi
Ω	&#937;	&Omega;	Omega
α	&#945;	&alpha;	alpha
β	&#946;	&beta;	beta
γ	&#947;	&gamma;	gamma
δ	&#948;	&delta;	delta

ε	&#949;	&epsilon;	epsilon
ζ	&#950;	&zeta;	zeta
η	&#951;	&eta;	eta
θ	&#952;	&theta;	theta
ι	&#953;	&iota;	iota
κ	&#954;	&kappa;	kappa
λ	&#955;	&lambda;	lambda
μ	&#956;	&mu;	mu
ν	&#957;	&nu;	nu
ξ	&#958;	&xi;	xi
ο	&#959;	&omicron;	omicron
π	&#960;	&pi;	pi
ρ	&#961;	&rho;	rho
ς	&#962;	&sigmaf;	sigmaf
σ	&#963;	&sigma;	sigma
τ	&#964;	&tau;	tau
υ	&#965;	&upsilon;	upsilon
φ	&#966;	&phi;	phi
χ	&#967;	&chi;	chi
ψ	&#968;	&psi;	psi
ω	&#969;	&omega;	omega
ϑ	&#977;	&thetasym;	theta symbol
ϒ	&#978;	&upsih;	upsilon symbol
ϖ	&#982;	&piv;	pi symbol

Other Symbols

Symbol	Entity Code	Entity Name	Description
Œ	Œ	Œ	capital ligature OE
œ	œ	œ	small ligature oe
Š	Š	Š	capital S with caron
š	š	š	small S with caron
Ÿ	Ÿ	Ÿ	capital Y with diaeres
ƒ	ƒ	ƒ	f with hook
ˆ	ˆ	ˆ	modifier letter circumflex accent
˜	˜	˜	small tilde
			en space
			em space
			thin space
	‌	‌	zero width non-joiner
	‍	‍	zero width joiner
	‎	‎	left-to-right mark
	‏	‏	right-to-left mark
–	–	–	en dash
—	—	—	em dash
'	‘	‘	left single quotation mark
'	’	’	right single quotation mark
‚	‚	‚	single low-9 quotation mark
"	“	“	left double quotation mark
"	”	”	right double quotation mark

„	„	„	double low-9 quotation mark
†	†	†	dagger
‡	‡	‡	double dagger
•	•	•	bullet
…	…	…	horizontal ellipsis
‰	‰	‰	per mille
′	′	′	minutes
″	″	″	seconds
‹	‹	‹	single left angle quotation
›	›	›	single right angle quotation
‾	‾	‾	overline
€	€	€	euro
™	™	™	trademark
←	←	←	left arrow
↑	↑	↑	up arrow
→	→	→	right arrow
↓	↓	↓	down arrow
↔	↔	↔	left right arrow
↵	↵	↵	carriage return arrow
⌈	⌈	⌈	left ceiling
⌉	⌉	⌉	right ceiling
⌊	⌊	⌊	left floor
⌋	⌋	⌋	right floor
◊	◊	◊	lozenge
♠	♠	♠	spade

♣	&#9827;	&clubs;	club
♥	&#9829;	&hearts;	heart
♦	&#9830;	&diams;	diamond

HTML & CSS

Programming Guide

Appendix 06

Language Codes

06. Language Codes

Country	ISO Code
Abkhazian	AB
Afan (Oromo)	OM
Afar	AA
Afrikaans	AF
Albanian	SQ
Amharic	AM
Arabic	AR
Armenian	HY
Assamese	AS
Aymara	AY
Azerbaijani	AZ
Bashkir	BA
Basque	EU
Bengali; Bangla	BN
Bhutani	DZ
Bihari	BH
Bislama	BI
Breton	BR
Bulgarian	BG
Burmese	MY
Byelorussian	BE
Cambodian	KM

Country	ISO Code
Catalan	CA
Chinese	ZH
Corsican	CO
Croatian	HR
Czech	CS
Danish	DA
Dutch	NL
English	EN
Esperanto	EO
Estonian	ET
Faroese	FO
Fiji	FJ
Finnish	FI
French	FR
Frisian	FY
Galician	GL
Georgian	KA
German	DE
Greek	EL
Greenlandic	KL
Guarani	GN
Gujarati	GU

Hausa	HA		Lingala	LN
Hebrew	HE		Lithuanian	LT
Hindi	HI		Macedonian	MK
Hungarian	HU		Malagasy	MG
Icelandic	IS		Malay	MS
Indonesian	ID		Malayalam	ML
Interlingua	IA		Maltese	MT
Interlingue	IE		Maori	MI
Inuktitut	IU		Marathi	MR
Inupiak	IK		Moldavian	MO
Irish	GA		Mongolian	MN
Italian	IT		Nauru	NA
Japanese	JA		Nepali	NE
Javanese	JV		Norwegian	NO
Kannada	KN		Occitan	OC
Kashmiri	KS		Oriya	OR
Kazakh	KK		Pashto; Pushto	PS
Kinyarwanda	RW		Persian (Farsi)	FA
Kirghiz	KY		Polish	PL
Korean	KO		Portuguese	PT
Kurdish	KU		Punjabi	PA
Kurundi	RN		Quechua	QU
Laothian	LO		Rhaeto - Romance	RM
Latin	LA		Telugu	TE

Latvian; Lettish	LV		Thai	TH
Samoan	SM		Romanian	RO
Sangho	SG		Russian	RU
Sanskrit	SA		Tibetan	BO
Scots Gaelic	GD		Tigrinya	TI
Serbian	SR		Tonga	TO
Serbo - Croatian	SH		Tsonga	TS
Sesotho	ST		Turkish	TR
Setswana	TN		Turkmen	TK
Shona	SN		Twi	TW
Sindhi	SD		Uigur	UG
Singhalese	SI		Ukrainian	UK
Siswati	SS		Urdu	UR
Slovak	SK		Uzbek	UZ
Slovenian	SL		Vietnamese	VI
Somali	SO		Volapuk	VO
Spanish	ES		Welsh	CY
Sudanese	SU		Wolof	WO
Swahili	SW		Xhosa	XH
Swedish	SV		Yiddish	YI
Tagalog	TL		Yoruba	YO
Tajik	TG		Zhuang	ZA
Tamil	TA		Zulu	ZU
Tatar	TT			

HTML & CSS

Programming Guide

Appendix 07

Events

07. Events

Mouse Events

onclick Event	The event raised when the user clicks on an HTML control.
ondblclick Event	The event raised when the user double-clicks on an HTML control.
onmousedown Event	The event raised when the user presses a mouse button.
onmousemove Event	The event raised when the user moves the mouse pointer.
onmouseout Event	The event raised when the user moves the mouse pointer out from within an HTML control.
onmouseover Event	The event raised when the user moves the mouse pointer over an HTML control.
onmouseup Event	The event raised when the user releases the mouse button.

Key Board Events

onkeydown Event	The event raised when the user presses a key on the keyboard.
onkeypress Event	when the user presses a key on the keyboard. This event will be raised continually until the user releases the key.
onkeyup Event	The event raised when the user releases a key that had been pressed.

HTML Control Events

onblur Event	The event raised when an HTML control loses focus.

onchange Event	The event raised when an HTML control loses focus and its value has changed.
onfocus Event	The event raised when focus is set to the HTML control.
onreset Event	The event raised when the user resets a form.
onselect Event	The event raised when the user selects text in an HTML control.
onsubmit Event	The event raised when the user submits a form.

Window Events

onload Event	The event raised when the window has completed loading.
onresize Event	The event raised when the user resizes the window.
onunload Event	The event raised when the user exits a document.

HTML & CSS

Programming Guide

Appendix 08

Measurement Values

08. Measurement Values

Measurement Unit	Description
%	percentage
in	inch
cm	centimeter
mm	millimeter
em	1em is equal to the current font size. 2em means 2 times the size of the current font. E.g., if an element is displayed with a font of 12 pt, then '2em' is 24 pt. The 'em' is a very useful unit in CSS, since it can adapt automatically to the font that the reader uses.
ex	one ex is the x-height of a font (x-height is usually about half the font-size)
pt	point (1 pt is the same as 1/72 inch)
pc	pica (1 pc is the same as 12 points)
px	pixels (a dot on the computer screen)